MACHINE LEARNING
with PYTHON
PROGRAMMING

A Practical Guide to Building Intelligent Applications with Python

RICHARD D. CROWLEY

Table of Contents

Part I:

Foundations of Machine Learning and Python

CHAPTER 1

Introduction to Machine Learning and Python

Machine learning (ML) is rapidly transforming industries by enabling systems to learn from data without explicit programming.[1] This subfield of artificial intelligence (AI) empowers computers to identify patterns, make predictions, and automate complex tasks.[2] Python has emerged as the leading programming language for ML due to its simplicity, versatility, and extensive ecosystem of powerful libraries.[3]

Key concepts in ML include supervised learning (learning from labeled data), unsupervised learning (discovering patterns in unlabeled data), and reinforcement learning (learning through interaction with an environment).[4] The rise of ML is fueled by the availability of big data, increased computing power, and the development of sophisticated algorithms.[5]

Python's ease of use and rich libraries, such as NumPy (numerical computing), Pandas (data manipulation), Matplotlib (visualization), and Scikit-learn (machine learning algorithms), make it ideal for ML development.[6] Setting up a robust Python environment using Anaconda, Jupyter Notebooks, or IDEs is crucial for efficient workflow.[7]

By mastering the fundamentals of ML and Python, professionals can unlock the potential to build intelligent applications that drive innovation and solve real-world problems.

1.1 The Rise of Machine Learning: Concepts and Applications

Machine learning (ML) is no longer a futuristic concept; it's a present-day reality profoundly shaping industries and daily life.[1] It's a subfield of artificial intelligence (AI) that empowers computers to learn from data without explicit programming.[2] Understanding its rise requires grasping its core concepts and diverse applications.

Core Concepts:

- **Learning from Data:** At its heart, ML involves algorithms that learn patterns and relationships from data.[3] This contrasts with traditional programming, where explicit rules are defined.[4]
- **Algorithms and Models:** ML algorithms, like linear regression,

decision trees, and neural networks, create models that represent learned patterns.[5] These models are then used for prediction, classification, or other tasks.[6]

- **Supervised, Unsupervised, and Reinforcement Learning:**
  - **Supervised Learning:** The algorithm learns from labeled data, where inputs are paired with correct outputs.[7] Examples include image classification and spam detection.[8]
  - **Unsupervised Learning:** The algorithm explores unlabeled data to discover hidden patterns or structures.[9] Examples include clustering and dimensionality reduction.[10]
  - **Reinforcement Learning:** The algorithm learns by interacting with an environment, receiving rewards or penalties for its actions.[11]

Examples include game playing and robotics.

- **Feature Engineering:** This crucial step involves selecting, transforming, and creating features (input variables) that significantly impact model performance.[12]
- **Model Evaluation:** Rigorous evaluation is essential to assess model accuracy, generalization, and suitability for specific tasks.[13]

Factors Driving the Rise of Machine Learning:

- **Availability of Big Data:** The explosion of data generated by digital devices, sensors, and online platforms provides the fuel for ML algorithms.[14]
- **Increased Computing Power:** Advances in hardware, including GPUs and cloud computing, enable the processing of massive datasets and complex models.[15]

- **Algorithm Development:** Continuous research and innovation have led to the development of sophisticated and effective ML algorithms.[16]
- **Open-Source Libraries and Frameworks:** Libraries like scikit-learn, TensorFlow, and PyTorch have democratized ML, making it accessible to a broader audience.[17]

Applications Across Industries:

- **Healthcare:** Disease diagnosis, drug discovery, personalized medicine, and patient monitoring.[18]
- **Finance:** Fraud detection, risk assessment, algorithmic trading, and customer segmentation.[19]
- **Retail:** Recommendation systems, personalized marketing, inventory management, and customer behavior analysis.[20]

- **Transportation:** Autonomous vehicles, traffic prediction, route optimization, and logistics.[21]
- **Manufacturing:** Predictive maintenance, quality control, and process optimization.[22]
- **Natural Language Processing (NLP):** Sentiment analysis, chatbots, language translation, and text summarization.
- **Computer Vision:** Image recognition, object detection, and video analysis.
- **Cybersecurity:** Threat detection, anomaly detection, and intrusion prevention.[23]

The Impact of Machine Learning:

- **Automation:** ML automates repetitive tasks, freeing up human resources for more creative and strategic work.[24]

- **Personalization:** ML enables personalized experiences in various domains, from online shopping to entertainment.[25]
- **Decision Making:** ML provides data-driven insights that support better decision-making in complex scenarios.[26]
- **Innovation:** ML drives innovation by enabling the development of new products, services, and business models.[27]

1.2 Understanding Python for Data Science and Machine Learning

Python has emerged as the dominant programming language for data science and machine learning, thanks to its simplicity, versatility, and extensive ecosystem.[28]

Why Python?

- **Ease of Learning and Use:** Python's clean syntax and readability make it easy to learn, even for beginners.[29]
- **Extensive Libraries:** Python boasts a rich collection of libraries specifically designed for data science and ML:[30]
  - **NumPy:** For numerical computing and array manipulation.[31]
  - **Pandas:** For data manipulation and analysis.[32]
  - **Matplotlib and Seaborn:** For data visualization.[33]
  - **Scikit-learn:** For machine learning[34] algorithms and tools.[35]
  - **TensorFlow and PyTorch:** For deep learning.[36]
-
- **Large and Active Community:** Python has a vibrant and supportive

community that contributes to its growth and development.[37]

- **Cross-Platform Compatibility:** Python runs on various operating systems, making it highly portable.[38]
- **Integration with Other Languages:** Python can be easily integrated with other languages, such as C++ and Java, for performance optimization.[39]
- **Versatility:** Python's versatility extends beyond data science and ML, making it suitable for web development, scripting, and other applications.[40]

Essential Python Libraries:

- **NumPy:**
  - Provides powerful tools for working with arrays and matrices.
  - Offers efficient mathematical functions and operations.[41]

- o Forms the foundation for many other data science libraries.
- **Pandas:**
  - o Provides data structures like DataFrames and Series for data manipulation and analysis.[42]
  - o Simplifies data cleaning, filtering, and transformation.[43]
  - o Offers powerful tools for handling missing data and time series.[44]
- **Matplotlib and Seaborn:**
  - o Matplotlib is a comprehensive library for creating static, interactive, and animated visualizations.[45]
  - o Seaborn is based on Matplotlib, and provides a high-level interface for drawing attractive and informative statistical graphics.[4647]
- **Scikit-learn:**
  - o Provides a wide range of machine learning algorithms for

classification, regression, clustering, and dimensionality reduction.[4849]

- o Offers tools for model evaluation, hyperparameter tuning, and data preprocessing.
- o Is designed for ease of use and interoperability with other libraries.[50]

- **TensorFlow and PyTorch:**
  - o Powerful frameworks for building and training deep learning models.[51]
  - o Provide tools for automatic differentiation, GPU acceleration, and model deployment.
  - o Tensorflow is backed by google, and Pytorch is backed by Meta.[52]

Setting Up the Python Environment:

- **Anaconda:** A popular distribution that includes Python, essential libraries, and package management tools.[53]
- **Jupyter Notebooks:** An interactive environment for writing and executing Python code, creating visualizations, and documenting your work.[54]
- **Integrated Development Environments (IDEs):** Tools like PyCharm, VS Code, and Spyder provide advanced features for coding, debugging, and project management.[55]
- **Google Colaboratory:** A free jupyter notebook service that requires no setup and runs entirely in the cloud.

The Future of Python in Machine Learning:

Python's dominance in the field is likely to continue, driven by its ongoing development, active community, and growing ecosystem. As ML evolves, Python will remain a crucial tool for researchers, developers, and practitioners.[56]

By understanding the concepts of machine learning and mastering Python's powerful libraries, you can unlock the potential to build intelligent applications that solve real-world problems.

1.3 Setting Up Your Python Environment (Anaconda, Jupyter Notebooks, IDEs)

A robust and efficient development environment is crucial for any machine learning practitioner. Let's explore the key components:

1. Anaconda: The All-in-One Distribution

- **What is Anaconda?** Anaconda is a free and open-source distribution of

Python and R programming languages for data science and machine learning.[1] It simplifies package management and deployment.

- **Why Anaconda?**
  - **Pre-installed Packages:** It comes with a vast collection of popular data science libraries (NumPy, Pandas, Scikit-learn, etc.), eliminating the need for manual installation.
  - **Conda Package Manager:** Conda allows you to easily install, update, and manage packages and dependencies, ensuring compatibility.
  - **Virtual Environments:** Anaconda facilitates the creation of isolated virtual environments, preventing conflicts between different project dependencies.
  - **Cross-Platform:** It's available for Windows, macOS, and Linux.

- **Installation:** Download the Anaconda installer from the official website (anaconda.com) and follow the installation instructions for your operating system.
- **Anaconda Navigator:** A graphical user interface (GUI) that provides access to Anaconda applications, environments, and packages.

2. Jupyter Notebooks: Interactive Computing

- **What are Jupyter Notebooks?** Jupyter Notebooks are web-based interactive computational environments that allow you to create and share documents containing live code, equations, visualizations, and narrative text.[2]
- **Why Jupyter Notebooks?**
  - **Interactive Coding:** Execute code cells interactively and see the results immediately.

- ○ **Data Visualization:** Embed visualizations directly within the notebook.
- ○ **Documentation:** Combine code with rich text, Markdown, and mathematical equations for clear documentation.
- ○ **Collaboration:** Share notebooks with others for collaboration and reproducibility.
- ○ **Exploratory Data Analysis (EDA):** Ideal for EDA, prototyping, and experimentation.
- **Launching Jupyter Notebooks:** After installing Anaconda, you can launch Jupyter Notebooks from the Anaconda Navigator or by typing jupyter notebook in the command prompt or terminal.
- **JupyterLab:** Is the next generation of Jupyter Notebooks, and provides a more powerful and flexible interface.

3. Integrated Development Environments (IDEs): Advanced Coding

- **What are IDEs?** IDEs are software applications that provide comprehensive facilities to computer programmers for software development.
- **Popular IDEs for Python:**
  - **PyCharm:** A powerful IDE developed by JetBrains, offering advanced features like code completion, debugging, and version control integration.
  - **Visual Studio Code (VS Code):** A lightweight and versatile code editor with extensive extensions for Python development.
  - **Spyder:** An open-source IDE designed specifically for scientific computing and data science.

- **Why use an IDE?**
  - **Code Completion and IntelliSense:** Provides intelligent code suggestions and error detection.
  - **Debugging:** Offers powerful debugging tools to identify and fix errors.
  - **Version Control:** Integrates with version control systems like Git.
  - **Project Management:** Facilitates the organization and management of large projects.
  - **Refactoring:** Provides tools to restructure code for improved readability and maintainability.
- **Choice of Environment:** Jupyter Notebooks are excellent for interactive exploration and prototyping, while IDEs are preferred for larger projects and production-level development.

1.4 Essential Python Libraries: NumPy, Pandas, Matplotlib, and Scikit-learn

These libraries form the foundation of most Python-based machine learning workflows.

1. NumPy: Numerical Computing Powerhouse

- **Purpose:** NumPy (Numerical Python) is the fundamental package for numerical computing in Python.
- **Key Features:**
  - **ndarray:** Provides a powerful N-dimensional array object for storing and manipulating numerical data.
  - **Mathematical Functions:** Offers a wide range of mathematical functions for array operations.

- ○ **Linear Algebra:** Supports linear algebra operations like matrix multiplication and eigenvalue decomposition.
- ○ **Random Number Generation:** Provides tools for generating random numbers and distributions.
- **Importance:** NumPy arrays are the basis for data representation in other libraries like Pandas and Scikit-learn.

2. Pandas: Data Manipulation and Analysis

- **Purpose:** Pandas provides high-performance, easy-to-use data structures and data analysis tools.
- **Key Features:**
  - ○ **DataFrame:** A 2D labeled data structure with columns of potentially different types, similar to a spreadsheet or SQL table.

- Series: A 1D labeled array capable of holding any data type.
- Data Cleaning and Transformation: Offers tools for handling missing data, filtering, sorting, and merging data.
- Data Loading and Saving: Supports reading and writing data from various formats (CSV, Excel, SQL, etc.).

- **Importance:** Pandas simplifies data preprocessing and exploration, making it essential for machine learning.

3. Matplotlib: Data Visualization

- **Purpose:** Matplotlib is a comprehensive library for creating static, animated, and interactive visualizations in Python.
- **Key Features:**[3]

- ○ **Plots and Charts:** Provides a wide range of plot types, including line plots, scatter plots, bar charts, histograms, and more.
- ○ **Customization:** Allows for extensive customization of plot appearance.
- ○ **Subplots:** Enables the creation of multiple plots within a single figure.
-

- **Importance:** Matplotlib is crucial for visualizing data patterns and model results.

4. Scikit-learn: Machine Learning Toolkit

- **Purpose:** Scikit-learn is a simple and efficient tool for data mining and data analysis.
- **Key Features:**

- **Machine Learning Algorithms:** Provides a wide range of supervised and unsupervised learning algorithms.
- **Model Evaluation:** Offers tools for evaluating model performance.
- **Data Preprocessing:** Includes tools for data scaling, feature selection, and dimensionality reduction.
- **Model Selection:** Supports hyperparameter tuning and model selection.

- **Importance:** Scikit-learn is the go-to library for building and evaluating machine learning models in Python.

1.5 A First Look: Building a Simple Machine Learning Model in Python

Let's illustrate a basic machine learning workflow using Scikit-learn:

Example: Linear Regression

1. **Import Libraries:**
2. Python

```
import numpy as np
import matplotlib.pyplot as plt
from sklearn.linear_model import LinearRegression
from sklearn.model_selection import train_test_split
from sklearn.metrics import mean_squared_error
```

3.

4.
5. **Generate Sample Data:**
6. Python

```python
X = 2 * np.random.rand(100, 1)
y = 4 + 3 * X + np.random.randn(100, 1)
```

7.
8.
9. **Split Data:**
10.   Python

```python
X_train, X_test, y_train, y_test = train_test_split(X, y, test_size=0.2, random_state=42)
```

11.
12.
13. **Create and Train the Model:**
14. Python

```
model = LinearRegression()
model.fit(X_train, y_train)
```

15.
16.
17. **Make Predictions:**
18.   Python

```
y_pred = model.predict(X_test)
```

19.
20.
21. **Evaluate the Model:**
22.   Python

```
mse = mean_squared_error(y_test, y_pred)
print(f"Mean Squared Error: {mse}")
```

23.
24.

25. **Visualize the Results:**
26. Python


```
plt.scatter(X_test, y_test)
plt.plot(X_test, y_pred, color='red')
plt.show()
```


27.
28.

This example demonstrates a simple linear regression model. From this foundation, you can build increasingly complex and powerful machine learning applications.

CHAPTER 2

Data Preprocessing and Exploration

This crucial phase in machine learning involves transforming raw data into a clean, usable format and gaining initial insights. Preprocessing tackles issues like missing values, outliers, and inconsistencies, ensuring data quality. Exploration uses statistical analysis and visualizations to understand data distributions, relationships, and potential features, laying the foundation for effective model building.

2.1 Data Acquisition and Loading (CSV, JSON, Databases)

Before any machine learning model can be built, data must be acquired and loaded into a format suitable for analysis.[1] This step involves identifying relevant data sources and understanding the various data formats.[2]

Data Acquisition:

- **Internal Data:** Data generated within an organization, such as sales records, customer databases, and sensor data.[3]
- **External Data:** Data obtained from external sources, such as public datasets, APIs, and web scraping.[4]
- **Web Scraping:** Extracting data from websites, often used when APIs are not available.[5]

- **APIs (Application Programming Interfaces):** Accessing data from services through structured requests.[6]
- **Public Datasets:** Repositories like Kaggle, UCI Machine Learning Repository, and data.gov provide a wealth of datasets for practice and research.[7]

Data Loading:

- **CSV (Comma-Separated Values):**
  - A simple and widely used format for storing tabular data.[8]
  - Pandas provides the read_csv() function to load CSV files into DataFrames.
  - Example:
  - Python

```
import pandas as pd
```

```
data = pd.read_csv('data.csv')
```

- ○
- ○
- ○ Considerations: Handling delimiters, encoding, and missing values.[9]
- **JSON (JavaScript Object Notation):**
  - ○ A lightweight data-interchange format that is easy for humans to read and write.[10]
  - ○ Pandas provides the read_json() function to load JSON data into DataFrames.
  - ○ Example:
  - ○ Python

```
data = pd.read_json('data.json')
```

- ○
- ○
- ○ Considerations: Nested JSON structures may require flattening or normalization.[11]
- **Databases (SQL, NoSQL):**
  - ○ Structured data stored in relational databases (SQL) or non-relational databases (NoSQL).
  - ○ Pandas can connect to SQL databases using libraries like sqlalchemy and execute SQL queries to retrieve data.
  - ○ Example:
  - ○ Python

```
from sqlalchemy import create_engine
engine                                    =
create_engine('sqlite:///mydatabase.db')
data = pd.read_sql_table('mytable', engine)
```

- ○
- ○
- ○ NoSQL databases like MongoDB can be accessed using libraries like pymongo.
- ○ Considerations: Database connection management, query optimization, and data retrieval.
- **Excel Files:**
  - ○ Pandas can also load excel files using the read_excel() function.
  - ○ Considerations: multiple sheets, and formatting.

2.2 Data Cleaning: Handling Missing Values, Outliers, and Inconsistent Data

Raw data is rarely clean and ready for analysis. Data cleaning is a critical step to ensure data quality and improve model performance.[12]

1. Handling Missing Values:

- **Identification:**
  - Use isnull() or isna() to identify missing values in DataFrames.
  - Visualize missing values using libraries like missingno.
- **Strategies:**
  - **Deletion:**
    - Remove rows or columns with a high percentage of missing values.
    - Use dropna() to remove rows or columns.
    - Considerations: Potential loss of valuable information.
  - **Imputation:**
    - Replace missing values with estimated values.

- **Mean/Median Imputation:** Replace missing values with the mean or median of the column.[13]
  - Use fillna(data.mean()) or fillna(data.median()).

- ■

- **Mode Imputation:** Replace missing values with the most frequent value.[14]
  - Use fillna(data.mode()[0]).

- ■

- **Forward/Backward Fill:** Propagate the last valid observation forward or backward.[15]

- Use
  fillna(method='ffill')
  or
  fillna(method='bfill')
  .

■

- **Interpolation:** Estimate missing values using interpolation techniques.[16]
    - Use interpolate().

■

- **Predictive Imputation:** Use machine learning models to predict missing values.
    - Libraries like scikit-learn and impyute can be used.
  - Considerations: Choosing the appropriate imputation method depends on the data distribution and the nature of missingness.

2. Handling Outliers:

- **Identification:**
  - Visualize data using box plots, scatter plots, and histograms to identify outliers.
  - Use statistical methods like z-scores or IQR (interquartile range) to detect outliers.[17]
- **Strategies:**
  - **Removal:**
    - Remove outliers that are clearly erroneous or irrelevant.
    - Considerations: Potential loss of valid data points.
  - **Transformation:**
    - Transform data to reduce the impact of outliers.
    - **Log Transformation:** Reduce skewness and the effect of extreme values.[18]

- **Winsorization:** Replace extreme values with values at a specific percentile.[19]
- Considerations: Choosing the appropriate transformation depends on the data distribution.

- **Capping/Flooring:**
  - Replace outliers with a maximum or minimum value.
  - Considerations: Simple, but can distort the data.
- **Treating Outliers as Missing Values:**
  - Treating outliers as missing values, and then applying missing value imputation techniques.
- Considerations: Outliers can carry important information, so careful analysis is crucial.[20]

3. Handling Inconsistent Data:

- **Data Type Conversion:**
  - Ensure data types are consistent and appropriate.
  - Use astype() to convert data types.
- **String Formatting:**
  - Standardize string formatting (e.g., capitalization, spacing).
  - Use string manipulation functions to clean and normalize text data.[21]
- **Date/Time Formatting:**
  - Convert date/time strings to datetime objects.[22]
  - Use pd.to_datetime() to parse date/time strings.
- **Duplicate Data:**
  - Identify and remove duplicate rows.
  - Use duplicated() and drop_duplicates() to handle duplicates.

- **Data Validation:**
  - Implement data validation rules to ensure data quality.
  - Use assertions or custom functions to check data integrity.

Importance of Data Cleaning:

- **Improved Model Accuracy:** Clean data leads to more accurate and reliable models.[23]
- **Reduced Bias:** Clean data helps reduce bias in models.[24]
- **Enhanced Data Quality:** Clean data improves the overall quality and consistency of the dataset.[25]
- **Faster Model Training:** Clean data can lead to faster model training times.[26]
- **Better Insights:** Clean data enables more accurate and meaningful insights from the data.[27]

Data preprocessing is a fundamental step in any machine learning project. By mastering data acquisition, loading, and cleaning techniques, you can ensure that your data is ready for analysis and model building.

2.3 Exploratory Data Analysis (EDA): Visualizations and Statistical Analysis

EDA is the process of analyzing and summarizing datasets to gain insights, understand patterns, and formulate hypotheses.[1] It's a crucial step before building any machine learning model.

Goals of EDA:

- **Understand Data Structure:** Identify data types, distributions, and relationships between variables.[2]
- **Detect Anomalies:** Identify outliers, missing values, and inconsistencies.[3]

- **Generate Hypotheses:** Formulate hypotheses about the data and potential relationships.[4]
- **Guide Feature Engineering:** Identify relevant features and inform feature engineering strategies.
- **Validate Assumptions:** Check if the data meets the assumptions of the chosen machine learning algorithms.[5]

Techniques for EDA:

- **Descriptive Statistics:**
  - **Summary Statistics:** Calculate mean, median, standard deviation, quartiles, and other descriptive statistics using describe() in Pandas.
  - **Frequency Distributions:** Analyze the distribution of categorical variables using value counts.[6]
  - **Correlation Analysis:** Calculate correlation coefficients

(e.g., Pearson, Spearman) to identify relationships between numerical variables using corr() in Pandas.

- **Covariance:** Measure the joint variability of two random variables.

- **Data Visualization:**
  - **Histograms:** Visualize the distribution of numerical variables using hist() in Matplotlib or Seaborn.
  - **Box Plots:** Identify outliers and visualize the distribution of numerical variables using boxplot() in Seaborn.
  - **Scatter Plots:** Visualize the relationship between two numerical variables using scatter() in Matplotlib or scatterplot() in Seaborn.
  - **Bar Charts:** Visualize the frequency or proportion of categorical variables using bar()

in Matplotlib or barplot() in Seaborn.

- o **Pie Charts:** Visualize the proportion of categorical variables using pie() in Matplotlib.
- o **Heatmaps:** Visualize the correlation matrix or other matrix data using heatmap() in Seaborn.
- o **Pair Plots:** Visualize pairwise relationships between multiple variables using pairplot() in Seaborn.
- o **Violin Plots:** Visualize the distribution of numerical data across different categories using violinplot() in Seaborn.
- o **Count Plots:** Visualize the count of observations in each category using countplot() in Seaborn.
- o **Time Series Plots:** If you have time series data, plot the data

over time to identify trends and seasonality.[7]

- **Grouped Analysis:**
  - ○ **Pivot Tables:** Summarize data by grouping variables using pivot_table() in Pandas.
  - ○ **Groupby Operations:** Calculate summary statistics for groups of data using groupby() in Pandas.
- **Hypothesis Testing:**
  - ○ **T-tests:** Compare the means of two groups.[8]
  - ○ **ANOVA:** Compare the means of multiple groups.
  - ○ **Chi-square Tests:** Analyze the association between categorical variables.[9]

2.4 Feature Engineering: Creating and Transforming Features for Better Models

Feature engineering is the process of creating and transforming features (input variables) to improve the performance of machine learning models.[10] It requires domain knowledge, creativity, and experimentation.

Importance of Feature Engineering:

- **Improved Model Accuracy:** Well-engineered features can significantly improve model accuracy.[11]
- **Faster Model Training:** Relevant features can reduce model complexity and training time.[12]
- **Enhanced Model Interpretability:** Engineered features can provide insights into the underlying relationships in the data.[13]

Techniques for Feature Engineering:

- **Creating New Features:**
  - **Polynomial Features:** Create polynomial combinations of existing features using PolynomialFeatures in Scikit-learn.
  - **Interaction Features:** Create interaction terms by multiplying or dividing existing features.
  - **Binning:** Discretize numerical features into bins or categories.
  - **Extracting Date/Time Features:** Extract features like day of the week, month, or year from date/time variables.
  - **Text Features:** Extract features from text data using techniques like TF-IDF or word embeddings.[14]
- **Transforming Features:**
  - **Log Transformation:** Apply a logarithmic transformation to

reduce skewness and the effect of outliers.[15]

- **Square Root Transformation:** Apply a square root transformation to reduce skewness.
- **Power Transformation:** Apply a power transformation to make the data more normally distributed.
- **One-Hot Encoding:** Convert categorical variables into numerical variables using one-hot encoding.[16]
- **Label Encoding:** Convert categorical variables into numerical variables using label encoding.[17]
- **Feature Splitting:** Split features into multiple features based on patterns.

- **Feature Selection:**
  - **Filter Methods:** Select features based on statistical

measures like correlation or mutual information.

- ○ **Wrapper Methods:** Select features based on the performance of a machine learning model.
- ○ **Embedded Methods:** Select features as part of the model training process (e.g., LASSO regression).
- ○ **Dimensionality Reduction:** Techniques like PCA to reduce the number of features.[18]
- **Handling Categorical Data:**
  - ○ **One-Hot Encoding:** Convert categorical variables into binary vectors.[19]
  - ○ **Label Encoding:** Convert categorical variables into numerical labels.
  - ○ **Target Encoding:** Replace categorical values with the mean of the target variable.

○ **Embedding:** Represent categorical variables as dense vectors.[20]

2.5 Data Scaling and Normalization Techniques

Data scaling and normalization are essential preprocessing steps to ensure that features are on a similar scale, which can improve the[21] performance of many machine learning algorithms.[22]

Why Scale and Normalize?

- **Improve Model Convergence:** Gradient descent-based algorithms converge faster when features are on a similar scale.[23]
- **Prevent Feature Domination:** Features with larger scales can dominate the learning process.[24]

- **Improve Model Stability:** Scaling and normalization can make models more stable and robust.[25]
- **Distance Based Algorithms:** Algorithms using distance calculations like K-Nearest Neighbors, and K-means clustering are highly impacted by feature scaling.[26]

Techniques for Scaling and Normalization:

- **Standardization (Z-score Normalization):**
  - Scales features to have a mean of 0 and a standard deviation of 1.
  - Formula: $z = (x - \mu) / \sigma$
  - Use StandardScaler in Scikit-learn.
- **Min-Max Scaling:**
  - Scales features to a specific range (e.g., [0, 1]).
  - Formula: $x\_scaled = (x - min(x)) / (max(x) - min(x))$

- Use MinMaxScaler in Scikit-learn.
- **Robust Scaling:**
  - Scales features using the median and interquartile range (IQR), making it robust to outliers.[27]
  - Use RobustScaler in Scikit-learn.
- **Normalization (Unit Vector Scaling):**
  - Scales features to have a unit norm (length of 1).
  - Use Normalizer in Scikit-learn.
- **Quantile Transformer:**
  - Transforms features to a uniform or normal distribution.
  - Use QuantileTransformer in Scikit-learn.
- **Power Transformer:**
  - Applies a power transformation to make the data more normally distributed.
  - Use PowerTransformer in Scikit-learn.

Choosing the Right Technique:

- **Standardization:** Suitable for most algorithms, especially those that assume normally distributed data.[28]
- **Min-Max Scaling:** Useful when features need to be within a specific range.
- **Robust Scaling:** Recommended when dealing with outliers.
- **Normalization:** Useful for text data or when the direction of the data is important.
- **Quantile/Power Transformer:** Useful when attempting to normalize data that has non-gaussian distributions.

EDA, feature engineering, and data scaling/normalization are essential steps in the machine learning pipeline.[29] By mastering these techniques, you can improve the quality of your data, build more accurate models, and gain deeper insights from your data.

CHAPTER 3

Fundamental Machine Learning Algorithms

These algorithms form the core of machine learning, enabling computers to learn from data. They include:

- **Linear Regression:** Predicts continuous values by fitting a linear relationship.
- **Logistic Regression:** Predicts categorical outcomes by estimating probabilities.
- **K-Nearest Neighbors (KNN):** Classifies or predicts based on the majority or average of nearby data points.
- **Decision Trees:** Partitions data into subsets based on feature values to make predictions.

These algorithms serve as building blocks for more complex models and are essential for understanding the principles of machine learning.

3.1 Supervised Learning: Regression and Classification Overview

Supervised learning is a type of machine learning where an algorithm learns from labeled data, meaning the input data is paired with corresponding correct outputs.[1] The goal is to build a model that can predict the output for new, unseen input data. Supervised learning can be broadly categorized into two main types: regression and classification.[2]

Regression:

- **Purpose:** Regression algorithms predict continuous numerical values.[3]

- **Examples:** Predicting house prices, stock market trends, or temperature.[4]
- **Key Characteristics:**
  - The output variable is a real number.
  - The goal is to minimize the difference between predicted and actual values.
  - Common evaluation metrics include Mean Squared Error (MSE), Root Mean Squared Error (RMSE), and R-squared.[5]

Classification:

- **Purpose:** Classification algorithms predict categorical labels or classes.[6]
- **Examples:** Identifying spam emails, classifying images, or predicting customer churn.[7]
- **Key Characteristics:**
  - The output variable is a discrete category.

- o The goal is to correctly assign input data to the appropriate class.
- o Common evaluation metrics include accuracy, precision, recall, and F1-score.[8]
- **Types:**
  - o **Binary Classification:** Two possible outcomes (e.g., spam/not spam).[9]
  - o **Multiclass Classification:** More than two possible outcomes (e.g., classifying different types of animals).[10]

General Supervised Learning Process:

1. **Data Collection:** Gather labeled data relevant to the problem.[11]
2. **Data Preprocessing:** Clean, transform, and prepare the data for modeling.

3. **Model Selection:** Choose an appropriate regression or classification algorithm.
4. **Model Training:** Train the model using the training data.
5. **Model Evaluation:** Evaluate the model's performance using test data.
6. **Model Deployment:** Deploy the trained model for making predictions on new data.

3.2 Linear Regression: Concepts, Implementation, and Evaluation

Linear regression is a fundamental and widely used supervised learning algorithm for regression tasks.[12] It models the relationship between a dependent variable (target) and one or more independent variables (features) by fitting a linear equation to the observed[13] data.[14]

Concepts:

- **Linear Equation:** In simple linear regression (one feature), the equation is: $y = mx + c$, where:
  - y is the predicted value.
  - x is the input feature.
  - m is the slope (coefficient) of the line.
  - c is the y-intercept.
- **Multiple Linear Regression:** When there are multiple features, the equation becomes: $y = b_0 + b_1x_1 + b_2x_2 + \ldots + b_nx_n$, where:
  - b_0 is the intercept.
  - $b_1, b_2, \ldots, b_n$ are the coefficients for each feature.
  - $x_1, x_2, \ldots, x_n$ are the input features.
- **Least Squares Method:** Linear regression aims to find the best-fitting line by minimizing the sum of the squared differences between the predicted and actual values.[15]
- **Assumptions:**

- Linearity: The relationship between features and target is linear.
- Independence: Features are independent of each other.
- Normality: Errors are normally distributed.
- Homoscedasticity: Errors have constant variance.

Implementation:

- Python's Scikit-learn library provides the LinearRegression class for easy implementation.
- The fit() method trains the model on the data, and the predict() method makes predictions.
- Example of implementation and evaluation of the model, is given in the previous response.

Evaluation:

- **Mean Squared Error (MSE):** Measures the average squared difference between predicted and actual values.[16] Lower values indicate better performance.[17]
- **Root Mean Squared Error (RMSE):** The square root of MSE, providing a measure in the same units as the target variable.[18]
- **R-squared (Coefficient of Determination):** Measures the proportion of variance in the target variable that is explained by the model.[19] Higher values (closer to 1) indicate a better fit.
- **Adjusted R-squared:** Modifies R-squared to account for the number of features in the model.[20]
- **Residual Analysis:** Examining the residuals (differences between predicted and actual values) can reveal

patterns or violations of assumptions.[21]

Applications:

- Predicting sales based on advertising spending.[22]
- Forecasting stock prices.
- Estimating housing prices based on features like size and location.[23]
- Analyzing trends in various fields like economics, finance, and healthcare.[24]

Importance:

- Linear regression is a simple yet powerful algorithm that provides a foundation for understanding more complex models.[25]
- It's interpretable, allowing you to understand the relationship between features and the target variable.

- It's widely used in various fields due to its effectiveness and ease of implementation.[26]

By understanding the concepts, implementation, and evaluation of linear regression, you can build a strong foundation for exploring more advanced machine learning algorithms.

3.3 Logistic Regression: Binary and Multiclass Classification

Logistic regression, despite its name, is a classification algorithm used to predict the probability of a binary or multiclass outcome.[1] It's a powerful tool for various classification tasks.

Binary Logistic Regression:

- **Purpose:** Predicts the probability of a binary outcome (e.g., 0 or 1, true or false).[2]
- **Sigmoid Function:** Uses the sigmoid function (logistic function) to transform the linear combination of features into a probability between 0 and 1.[3]
  - Formula: $sigmoid(z) = 1 / (1 + e^{(-z)})$, where z is the linear combination of features.

-
- **Decision Boundary:** Classifies data points based on a decision boundary, typically set at 0.5.[4] If the probability is greater than 0.5, the data point is classified as 1; otherwise, it's classified as 0.[5]
- **Cost Function:** Uses the logistic loss function (cross-entropy loss) to measure the error between predicted and actual probabilities.

- **Implementation:** Scikit-learn's LogisticRegression class provides easy implementation.
- **Evaluation:** Common metrics include accuracy, precision, recall, F1-score, and ROC-AUC.[6]

Multiclass Logistic Regression:

- **Purpose:** Predicts the probability of multiple classes (e.g., classifying different types of fruits).[7]
- **Softmax Function:** Uses the softmax function to transform the linear combination of features into a probability distribution over multiple classes.[8]
  - Formula: $\text{softmax}(z\_i) = e^{\wedge}(z\_i) / \Sigma e^{\wedge}(z\_j)$, where z_i is the linear combination for class i.
-
- **One-vs-Rest (OvR) or One-vs-All (OvA):** Trains multiple binary logistic

regression classifiers, one for each class versus all other classes.

- **Multinomial Logistic Regression:** Directly models the probabilities of multiple classes.
- **Implementation:** Scikit-learn's LogisticRegression class supports multiclass classification using OvR or multinomial methods.
- **Evaluation:** Common metrics include accuracy, precision, recall, F1-score (macro, micro, weighted), and confusion matrix.

Applications:

- Spam detection.
- Medical diagnosis.
- Customer churn prediction.
- Image classification.
- Natural language processing (NLP) tasks.

3.4 K-Nearest Neighbors (KNN): Classification and Regression

KNN is a simple and versatile algorithm used for both classification and regression tasks.[9] It's a non-parametric and instance-based learning algorithm.

Classification:

- **Purpose:** Classifies a data point based on the majority class of its k-nearest neighbors.
- **Distance Metrics:** Uses distance metrics like Euclidean distance, Manhattan distance, or Minkowski distance to find the nearest neighbors.
- **Choosing K:** The value of k is a crucial parameter. A small k can lead to overfitting, while a large k can lead to underfitting.

- **Implementation:** Scikit-learn's KNeighborsClassifier class provides easy implementation.
- **Evaluation:** Common metrics include accuracy, precision, recall, F1-score, and confusion matrix.

Regression:

- **Purpose:** Predicts a continuous value based on the average or weighted average of the target values of its k-nearest neighbors.
- **Implementation:** Scikit-learn's KNeighborsRegressor class provides easy implementation.
- **Evaluation:** Common metrics include MSE, RMSE, and R-squared.

Key Characteristics:

- **Non-parametric:** Makes no assumptions about the underlying data distribution.
- **Instance-based:** Stores the training data and makes predictions based on the nearest neighbors.
- **Lazy Learning:** Doesn't build a model explicitly during the training phase.
- **Sensitive to Feature Scaling:** Feature scaling is crucial for KNN to perform well.
- **Computational Cost:** Can be computationally expensive for large datasets.

Applications:

- Recommendation systems.
- Image recognition.
- Anomaly detection.
- Financial forecasting.

3.5 Decision Trees: Building and Interpreting Tree-Based Models

Decision trees are powerful and interpretable algorithms used for both classification and regression tasks.[10] They partition the data into subsets based on feature values, creating a tree-like structure.[11]

Building Decision Trees:

- **Recursive Partitioning:** The algorithm recursively splits the data into subsets based on feature values, aiming to create subsets that are as pure as possible (i.e., contain data points from a single class).
- **Splitting Criteria:**
  - **Gini Impurity (Classification):** Measures the impurity of a node.[12]

- **Entropy (Classification):** Measures the disorder or randomness of a node.[13]
- **Mean Squared Error (Regression):** Measures the variance of the target variable in a node.

- **Stopping Criteria:**
  - Maximum depth of the tree.
  - Minimum number of samples required to split a node.
  - Minimum number of samples required at a leaf node.

Interpreting Decision Trees:

- **Tree Structure:** The tree structure provides a clear and intuitive representation of the decision-making process.[14]
- **Feature Importance:** Decision trees can provide insights into the

importance of features in predicting the target variable.

- **Decision Rules:** The paths from the root node to the leaf nodes represent decision rules.

Advantages:

- **Interpretability:** Easy to understand and visualize.
- **Handling Categorical and Numerical Data:** Can handle both types of data.
- **Feature Importance:** Provides insights into feature importance.
- **Non-linear Relationships:** Can model non-linear relationships.

Disadvantages:

- **Overfitting:** Prone to overfitting, especially with deep trees.

- **Instability:** Small changes in the data can lead to significant changes in the tree structure.
- **Bias:** Can be biased towards features with more categories.[15]

Implementation:

- Scikit-learn's DecisionTreeClassifier and DecisionTreeRegressor classes provide easy implementation.
- Visualization: graphviz library can be used to visualize decision trees.

Applications:

- Medical diagnosis.
- Credit risk assessment.
- Customer segmentation.
- Fraud detection.

By understanding logistic regression, KNN, and decision trees, you can build a strong foundation for tackling a wide range of classification and regression problems.

Part II:

Advanced Machine Learning Techniques

CHAPTER 4

Ensemble Methods: Boosting and Bagging

Ensemble methods enhance machine learning performance by combining multiple models.[1] **Bagging** (like Random Forests) reduces variance by training models independently on bootstrapped datasets and aggregating their predictions.[2] **Boosting** (like AdaBoost and Gradient Boosting) reduces bias by sequentially training models that correct the errors of previous ones.[3] Both techniques leverage the diversity of multiple learners to create a more robust and accurate final model.[4]

4.1 Understanding Ensemble Learning: Reducing Variance and Bias

Ensemble learning is a powerful technique in machine learning that combines multiple base models to improve overall predictive performance.[1] The underlying principle is that a collection of weak learners, when combined, can create a strong learner.[2]

Key Concepts:

- **Weak Learners:** Base models that perform slightly better than random guessing.[3] They are often simple models like decision trees with shallow depths.[4]
- **Strong Learners:** Ensemble models that achieve high accuracy and generalization.
- **Diversity:** The base models in an ensemble should be diverse, meaning

they should make different types of errors.[5] Diversity is crucial for the ensemble to outperform individual models.

- **Variance:** Variance refers to the variability of a model's predictions for different training datasets. High variance indicates that the model is sensitive to small fluctuations in the training data, leading to overfitting.[6]
- **Bias:** Bias refers to the error introduced by approximating a real-world problem, which may be complex, by a simplified model. High bias[7] can lead to underfitting.[8]

Goals of Ensemble Learning:

- **Reduce Variance:** Bagging techniques, like Random Forests, aim to reduce variance by averaging the predictions of multiple diverse models.[9]

- **Reduce Bias:** Boosting techniques, like AdaBoost and Gradient Boosting, aim to reduce bias by sequentially training models that correct the errors of previous models.[10]
- **Improve Generalization:** Ensemble methods can improve the generalization ability of models, making them more robust to unseen data.[11]

Types of Ensemble Methods:

- **Bagging (Bootstrap Aggregating):**
  - Trains multiple base models on different subsets of the training data, created by sampling with replacement (bootstrapping).[12]
  - Combines the predictions of the base models by averaging (regression) or voting (classification).[13]

- Reduces variance and improves stability.
- Example: Random Forests.
- **Boosting:**
  - Trains base models sequentially, with each model focusing on correcting the errors of the previous models.[14]
  - Assigns weights to training samples, giving more weight to misclassified samples.[15]
  - Reduces bias and improves accuracy.
  - Examples: AdaBoost, Gradient Boosting Machines (GBM), XGBoost, LightGBM, CatBoost.[16]
- **Stacking:**
  - Combines the predictions of multiple base models using another model (meta-learner).
  - The meta-learner learns how to best combine the predictions of the base models.[17]

○ Can achieve high accuracy but can be complex to implement.

4.2 Random Forests: Building Robust Models with Bagging

Random Forests are a powerful and widely used ensemble learning algorithm based on the bagging technique.[18] They are effective for both classification and regression tasks.

Key Concepts:

- **Decision Trees as Base Models:** Random Forests use decision trees as base models.[19]
- **Bootstrapping:** Creates multiple subsets of the training data by sampling with replacement.[20]
- **Random Feature Selection:** At each node of a decision tree, only a random subset of features is

considered for splitting.[21] This[22] introduces diversity among the trees.

- **Aggregation:** Combines the predictions of the individual decision trees by averaging (regression) or voting (classification).[23]

Building Random Forests:

1. **Bootstrap Sampling:** Create multiple bootstrap samples of the training data.
2. **Decision Tree Construction:** For each bootstrap sample, build a decision tree.
   - At each node, randomly select a subset of features.
   - Choose the best feature and split point based on a splitting criterion (e.g., Gini impurity, entropy).
   - Grow the tree without pruning (or with minimal pruning) to maximize diversity.

3. **Aggregation:** Combine the predictions of the individual decision trees.

- For classification, use majority voting.
- For regression, use averaging.

Advantages of Random Forests:

- **High Accuracy:** Random Forests often achieve high accuracy and generalization.[24]
- **Robustness to Overfitting:** Bagging and random feature selection reduce variance and prevent overfitting.[25]
- **Feature Importance:** Random Forests can provide insights into the importance of features.[26]
- **Handling Categorical and Numerical Data:** Can handle both types of data.

- **Parallelization:** Decision trees can be trained in parallel, making Random Forests efficient for large datasets.[27]
- **Minimal Data Preprocessing:** Random forests generally require less data cleaning.[28]

Disadvantages of Random Forests:

- **Interpretability:** Can be less interpretable than individual decision trees, especially with a large number of trees.
- **Computational Cost:** Can be computationally expensive for large datasets and a large number of trees.[29]
- **Memory Usage:** Can require significant memory to store the ensemble of trees.

Implementation:

- Scikit-learn's RandomForestClassifier and RandomForestRegressor classes provide easy implementation.
- Key parameters:
  - n_estimators: The number of trees in the forest.
  - max_features: The number of features to consider when looking for the best split.[30]
  - max_depth: The maximum depth of the trees.
  - min_samples_split: The minimum number of samples required to split an internal node.
  - min_samples_leaf: The minimum number[31] of samples required to be at a leaf node.[32]

Applications:

- Image classification.
- Medical diagnosis.

- Fraud detection.
- Financial forecasting.
- Recommendation systems.

By understanding ensemble learning and mastering Random Forests, you can build powerful and robust machine learning models that achieve high accuracy and generalization.

4.3 Gradient Boosting Machines (GBM): XGBoost, LightGBM, and CatBoost

Gradient Boosting Machines (GBMs) are a powerful family of boosting algorithms that build models in a stage-wise fashion, optimizing a loss function using gradient descent.[1] They are known for their high accuracy and flexibility.[2]

Key Concepts:

- **Sequential Training:** GBMs train base models sequentially, with each model focusing on correcting the errors of the previous models.[3]
- **Loss Function:** GBMs optimize a differentiable loss function (e.g., mean squared error, cross-entropy) to minimize the error between predicted and actual values.[4]
- **Gradient Descent:** GBMs use gradient descent to find the optimal parameters for each base model.[5]
- **Weak Learners:** GBMs typically use decision trees as weak learners.[6]

General GBM Process:

1. **Initialize Model:** Start with a simple model (e.g., a constant value).
2. **Calculate Residuals:** Calculate the residuals (differences between actual and predicted values).

3. **Train Base Model:** Train a base model (e.g., decision tree) to predict the residuals.
4. **Update Model:** Update the overall model by adding the predictions of the base model, scaled by a learning rate.[7]
5. **Repeat:** Repeat steps 2-4 for a specified number of iterations.

XGBoost (Extreme Gradient Boosting):

- **Purpose:** A highly optimized and scalable implementation of gradient boosting.
- **Key Features:**
  - **Regularization:** Includes L1 and L2 regularization to prevent overfitting.[8]
  - **Tree Pruning:** Uses tree pruning to control the complexity of the trees.[9]

- ○ **Parallel Processing:** Supports parallel processing for faster training.[10]
- ○ **Handling Missing Values:** Can handle missing values naturally.[11]
- ○ **Cache Optimization:** Uses cache optimization for efficient memory usage.[12]
- **Advantages:** High accuracy, fast training, and robustness.[13]
- **Applications:** Wide range of tasks, including classification, regression, and ranking.[14]

LightGBM (Light Gradient Boosting Machine):

- **Purpose:** A fast and efficient gradient boosting framework developed by Microsoft.
- **Key Features:**
  - ○ **Gradient-based One-Side Sampling (GOSS):** Samples

data points to reduce computational cost.[15]

- ○ **Exclusive Feature Bundling (EFB):** Bundles mutually exclusive features to reduce dimensionality.[16]
- ○ **Histogram-based Learning:** Uses histograms to bin continuous features, reducing memory usage and speeding up training.
- ○ **Leaf-wise Tree Growth:** Grows trees leaf-wise, resulting in deeper trees and better accuracy.
- **Advantages:** Faster training, lower memory usage, and high accuracy.
- **Applications:** Large-scale datasets and real-time applications.

CatBoost (Categorical Boosting):

- **Purpose:** A gradient boosting library that excels at handling categorical features.[17]
- **Key Features:**
  - **Ordered Target Statistics:** Uses ordered target statistics to handle categorical features, reducing overfitting.[18]
  - **Symmetric Trees:** Grows symmetric trees, resulting in faster training and better generalization.
  - **Handling Missing Values:** Can handle missing values naturally.[19]
  - **GPU Support:** Supports GPU acceleration for faster training.[20]
- **Advantages:** Excellent handling of categorical features, high accuracy, and robustness.[21]
- **Applications:** Datasets with many categorical features, such as e-commerce and marketing data.[22]

4.4 AdaBoost: Adaptive Boosting for Improved Accuracy

AdaBoost (Adaptive Boosting) is a boosting algorithm that adaptively adjusts the weights of training samples to focus on misclassified samples.[23]

Key Concepts:

- **Sequential Training:** AdaBoost trains base models sequentially, with each model focusing on correcting the errors of the previous models.[24]
- **Sample Weights:** AdaBoost assigns weights to training samples, giving more weight to misclassified samples.[25]
- **Weak Learners:** AdaBoost typically uses decision stumps (decision trees with one level) as weak learners.[26]
- **Adaptive Weights:** AdaBoost adjusts the weights of the training

samples at each iteration, giving more weight to misclassified samples.[27]

- **Final Prediction:** Combines the predictions of the base models by weighted voting.

AdaBoost Process:

1. **Initialize Weights:** Assign equal weights to all training samples.
2. **Train Base Model:** Train a base model on the training data with the current weights.
3. **Calculate Error:** Calculate the weighted error of the base model.
4. **Calculate Model Weight:** Calculate the weight of the base model based on its error.
5. **Update Sample Weights:** Update the weights of the training samples, giving more weight to misclassified samples.
6. **Repeat:** Repeat steps 2-5 for a specified number of iterations.

7. **Final Prediction:** Combine the predictions of the base models by weighted voting.

Advantages:

- **Improved Accuracy:** AdaBoost can significantly improve the accuracy of weak learners.[28]
- **Simplicity:** AdaBoost is relatively simple to implement and understand.[29]
- **Robustness:** AdaBoost is robust to outliers and noisy data.

Disadvantages:

- **Sensitivity to Noisy Data:** AdaBoost can be sensitive to noisy data and outliers.[30]
- **Overfitting:** AdaBoost can overfit if the base models are too complex or the number of iterations is too large.[31]

4.5 Evaluating and Tuning Ensemble Models

Evaluating and tuning ensemble models is crucial to ensure optimal performance and generalization.

Evaluation Metrics:

- **Classification:** Accuracy, precision, recall, F1-score, ROC-AUC, confusion matrix.
- **Regression:** Mean Squared Error (MSE), Root Mean Squared Error (RMSE), R-squared.

Evaluation Techniques:

- **Cross-Validation:** Use k-fold cross-validation to evaluate model performance and estimate generalization error.

- **Train-Test Split:** Split the data into training and test sets to evaluate model performance on unseen data.[32]

Hyperparameter Tuning:

- **Grid Search:** Exhaustively search over a predefined set of hyperparameter values.
- **Random Search:** Randomly sample hyperparameter values from a predefined distribution.[33]
- **Bayesian Optimization:** Use Bayesian optimization to efficiently search for optimal hyperparameter values.[34]
- **Hyperparameter Tuning Tools:** Optuna, Hyperopt, and Scikit-learn's GridSearchCV and RandomizedSearchCV.

Key Hyperparameters to Tune:

- **Number of Estimators (n_estimators):** The number of base models in the ensemble.
- **Learning Rate (learning_rate):** Controls the contribution of each base model to the overall model.[35]
- **Maximum Depth (max_depth):** Controls the complexity of the base models.[36]
- **Minimum Samples Split (min_samples_split):** Controls the minimum number of samples required to split a node.[37]
- **Minimum Samples Leaf (min_samples_leaf):** Controls the minimum number of samples required to be at a leaf node.[38]
- **Regularization Parameters (alpha, lambda):** Controls the regularization strength to prevent overfitting.[39]

Techniques to Improve Ensemble Performance:

- **Feature Engineering:** Create and transform features to improve model accuracy.
- **Feature Selection:** Select relevant features to reduce model complexity and improve generalization.
- **Early Stopping:** Stop training when the model's performance on a validation set stops improving.[40]
- **Model Stacking:** Combine multiple ensemble models using a meta-learner.[41]

By mastering GBMs, AdaBoost, and the techniques for evaluating and tuning ensemble models, you can build powerful and accurate machine learning solutions.

CHAPTER 5

Support Vector Machines (SVMs)

SVMs are powerful supervised learning models that excel in both classification and regression.[1] They aim to find the optimal hyperplane that maximizes the margin between different classes, enhancing generalization.[2] Key concepts include support vectors (crucial data points), the kernel trick (for handling non-linear data), and soft margins (allowing for some misclassification).[3] Linear SVMs are efficient for linearly separable data, while kernelized SVMs extend their capability to complex, non-linear problems.

5.1 Introduction to Support Vector Machines: Maximizing Margins

Support Vector Machines (SVMs) are a powerful and versatile class of supervised learning algorithms used for both classification and regression tasks.[1] Their core principle is to find an optimal hyperplane that best separates different classes in the feature space, maximizing the margin between them.[2]

Key Concepts:

- **Hyperplane:** In an n-dimensional space, a hyperplane is an (n-1)-dimensional subspace.[3] For example, in a 2D space, a hyperplane is a line; in a 3D space, it's a plane.[4]
- **Margin:** The margin is the distance between the hyperplane and the closest data points from each class.[5]

Maximizing the margin leads to better generalization and robustness.[6]

- **Support Vectors:** The data points that lie closest to the hyperplane and influence its position and orientation.[7] They are the critical elements that define the margin.

- **Optimal Hyperplane:** The hyperplane that maximizes the margin and minimizes the classification error.[8]

- **Kernel Trick:** A technique that maps the input data into a higher-dimensional space, where it becomes easier to find a linear separating hyperplane.[9] This allows SVMs to handle non-linear data.[10]

- **Soft Margin:** Allows some misclassifications to occur, providing flexibility when dealing with non-linearly separable data or noisy data.[11]

- **Regularization:** Controls the trade-off between maximizing the margin and minimizing the training error.

Maximizing Margins:

The goal of SVMs is to find the hyperplane that maximizes the margin.[12] A larger margin implies that the decision boundary is more robust, as it is less sensitive to small changes in the data.

- **Geometric Intuition:** Imagine two classes of data points separated by a line (in 2D).[13] The SVM aims to find the line that is as far away as possible from the closest points of both classes.[14]
- **Mathematical Formulation:** The margin is calculated as the distance between the support vectors and the hyperplane. The SVM optimization problem involves maximizing this distance while minimizing the classification error.

5.2 Linear SVMs: Classification and Regression

Linear SVMs are the simplest form of SVMs, where the separating hyperplane is a linear function of the input features.[15] They are effective when the data is linearly separable or can be approximated as linearly separable.

Linear SVMs for Classification:

- **Binary Classification:** Linear SVMs are primarily used for binary classification, where the goal is to separate data points into two classes.[16]
- **Hyperplane Equation:** The hyperplane is defined by the equation $w^T x + b = 0$, where w is the weight vector, x is the input feature vector, and b is the bias term.
- **Decision Function:** The decision function[17] is $f(x) = \text{sign}(w^T x + b)$. If $f(x)$ is positive, the data point is

classified as one class; if it's negative, it's classified as the other class.

- **Hard Margin SVM:** Assumes that the data is perfectly linearly separable and aims to find a hyperplane that completely separates the classes without any misclassifications.
- **Soft Margin SVM:** Allows some misclassifications to occur, providing flexibility when dealing with non-linearly separable data.[18] A regularization parameter (C) controls the trade-off between maximizing the margin and minimizing the training error.[19]
    - A high C value will attempt to classify all training examples correctly, which might overfit the data.
    - A low C value will allow more training errors, which might underfit the data.[20]
-

- **Implementation:** Scikit-learn's LinearSVC and SVC classes provide easy implementation. LinearSVC is optimized for linear kernels, and is faster than SVC(kernel='linear').

Linear SVMs for Regression:

- **Support Vector Regression (SVR):** Linear SVMs can also be used for regression tasks, where the goal is to predict a continuous numerical value.[21]
- **Epsilon-Insensitive Loss:** SVR uses an epsilon-insensitive loss function, which ignores errors within a certain range (epsilon).[22] This creates a tube around the predicted values, and errors outside the tube are penalized.
- **Hyperplane Equation:** The hyperplane is defined by the same equation as in classification: $w^T x + b = y$, where y is the predicted value.

- **Regularization:** A regularization parameter (C) controls the trade-off between fitting the data and minimizing the complexity of the model.[23]
- **Implementation:** Scikit-learn's LinearSVR and SVR classes provide easy implementation. LinearSVR is optimized for linear kernels.
- **Advantages of linear SVR:**
  - Effective in high dimensional spaces.
  - Memory efficient.
  - Effective when the number of dimensions is greater than the number of samples.[24]

Advantages of Linear SVMs:

- **Effective in High-Dimensional Spaces:** Linear SVMs can handle high-dimensional data efficiently.[25]

- **Memory Efficiency:** They use a subset of training points (support vectors) in the decision function, making them memory efficient.[26]
- **Interpretability:** Linear SVMs are relatively interpretable, as the weight vector provides insights into the importance of features.
- **Robustness:** Maximizing the margin makes linear SVMs robust to outliers.

Disadvantages of Linear SVMs:

- **Linear Separability Assumption:** They assume that the data is linearly separable, which may not always be the case.
- **Sensitivity to Feature Scaling:** Feature scaling is crucial for linear SVMs to perform well.
- **Computational Cost:** Training can be computationally expensive for large datasets.[27]

Applications:

- **Text Classification:** Categorizing documents or emails.
- **Image Classification:** Identifying objects in images.
- **Financial Forecasting:** Predicting stock prices or market trends.[28]
- **Medical Diagnosis:** Classifying diseases based on patient data.[29]

By understanding the principles of maximizing margins and the applications of linear SVMs, you can build powerful and robust models for a wide range of classification and regression tasks.

5.3 Kernel SVMs: Handling Non-Linear Data with Kernel Functions

One of the most powerful aspects of Support Vector Machines (SVMs) is their ability to handle non-linearly separable data through the use of kernel functions.[1]

The Challenge of Non-Linear Separability:

- In many real-world scenarios, data points from different classes cannot be separated by a simple linear hyperplane.
- Attempting to fit a linear SVM to such data would result in poor performance and underfitting.

The Kernel Trick:

- The kernel trick is a technique that implicitly maps the input data into a higher-dimensional feature space, where it becomes linearly separable.[2]
- Instead of explicitly computing the coordinates of the data points in the higher-dimensional space, kernel functions compute the inner products between the data points in this space.[3]
- This avoids the computational cost of explicitly mapping the data, which can be very high or even infinite-dimensional.
- Essentially, the kernel functions calculate the similarity between data points in the original space, as if they were in the higher dimensional space.

Common Kernel Functions:

- **Polynomial Kernel:**
  - Maps the data into a polynomial feature space.

- Suitable for data with polynomial relationships.[4]
- Formula: $K(x, x') = (x^T x' + c)^d$, where d is the degree of the polynomial and c is a constant.
- **Radial Basis Function (RBF) Kernel (Gaussian Kernel):**
  - Maps the data into an infinite-dimensional feature space.
  - Suitable for data with complex, non-linear relationships.
  - Formula: $K(x, x') = \exp(-\gamma ||x - x'||^2)$, where γ (gamma) controls the width of the Gaussian kernel.
- **Sigmoid Kernel:**
  - Maps the data into a hyperbolic tangent feature space.
  - Similar to a two-layer neural network.

○ Formula: $K(x, x') = \tanh(\alpha\, x^\wedge T\, x' + c)$, where α and c are constants.

Advantages of Kernel SVMs:

- **Handling Non-Linear Data:** Kernel functions enable SVMs to handle complex, non-linear relationships.
- **Flexibility:** Different kernel functions can be chosen based on the characteristics of the data.
- **Implicit Feature Mapping:** The kernel trick avoids the computational cost of explicitly mapping the data.[5]

5.4 SVM Parameter Tuning and Optimization

To achieve optimal performance with SVMs, it's crucial to tune the hyperparameters and optimize the model.

Key Hyperparameters:

- **C (Regularization Parameter):**
  - Controls the trade-off between maximizing the margin and minimizing the training error.
  - A small C value leads to a wider margin but allows more misclassifications (regularization).[6]
  - A large C value leads to a narrower margin and fewer misclassifications (less regularization).
- **Kernel Type:**

- Determines the type of kernel function used (e.g., linear, polynomial, RBF).
- **Gamma (γ) (RBF Kernel):**
  - Controls the width of the Gaussian kernel.
  - A small gamma value leads to a wider Gaussian kernel, capturing global patterns.
  - A large gamma value leads to a narrower Gaussian kernel, capturing local patterns.
- **Degree (d) (Polynomial Kernel):**
  - Controls the degree of the polynomial kernel.
- **Epsilon (ε) (SVR):**
  - Defines the epsilon-tube in which no penalty is associated in the training loss function with points predicted within a distance epsilon from the actual value.[7]

Parameter Tuning Techniques:

- **Grid Search:**
  - Exhaustively searches over a predefined set of hyperparameter values.
  - Evaluates the model's performance for each combination of hyperparameters.
  - Can be computationally expensive for large datasets and a wide range of hyperparameters.
- **Random Search:**
  - Randomly samples hyperparameter values from a predefined distribution.
  - Can be more efficient than grid search for high-dimensional hyperparameter spaces.
- **Cross-Validation:**

- Used to evaluate the model's performance and estimate generalization error.
- K-fold cross-validation is a common technique.
- **Bayesian Optimization:**
  - Uses Bayesian inference to find the optimal hyperparameters more efficiently than grid or random search.
  - Builds a probabilistic model of the objective function and uses it to guide the search.

Optimization Considerations:

- **Feature Scaling:** Scaling the features to a similar range is crucial for SVMs to perform well.
- **Data Preprocessing:** Cleaning and preprocessing the data can significantly impact model performance.[8]

- **Computational Cost:** Training SVMs can be computationally expensive, especially for large datasets.[9]

5.5 Applications of SVMs in Real-World Scenarios

SVMs have a wide range of applications in various fields due to their versatility and effectiveness.[10]

1. Image Classification:

- SVMs can be used to classify images based on their features, such as pixel values or extracted features.[11]
- Kernel SVMs are particularly effective for image classification tasks with complex, non-linear patterns.

2. Text Classification:

- SVMs can be used to classify text documents, such as emails, articles, or reviews, based on their content.[12]
- They are effective for sentiment analysis, spam detection, and topic classification.

3. Bioinformatics:

- SVMs are used in bioinformatics for tasks such as protein classification, gene expression analysis, and disease diagnosis.[13]
- Kernel SVMs can handle high-dimensional biological data.[14]

4. Financial Forecasting:

- SVMs can be used to predict stock prices, market trends, and financial risks.[15]
- They can capture complex, non-linear relationships in financial data.

5. Medical Diagnosis:

- SVMs can be used to diagnose diseases based on patient data, such as symptoms, medical images, and test results.[16]
- They can help improve the accuracy and efficiency of medical diagnosis.

6. Handwriting Recognition:

- SVMs are used to recognize handwritten characters and digits.[17]
- Their ability to handle complex patterns makes them suitable for this task.

7. Anomaly Detection:

- SVMs can be used to detect anomalies or outliers in data.[18]

- They can identify data points that deviate significantly from the normal pattern.

8. Pattern Recognition:

- SVMs are used in many pattern recognition tasks, such as speech recognition, face recognition, and signal processing.[19]

By understanding kernel SVMs, their parameter tuning, and real-world applications, you can leverage the power of SVMs to solve a wide range of machine learning problems.

CHAPTER 6

Clustering and Dimensionality Reduction

These unsupervised learning techniques are crucial for understanding unlabeled data.[1] **Clustering** groups similar data points, revealing hidden structures and patterns.[2] **Dimensionality Reduction** simplifies complex datasets by reducing the number of features, enhancing visualization, and improving model efficiency.[3] Both methods are vital for exploratory data analysis and preparing data for further machine learning tasks.[4]

6.1 Unsupervised Learning: Clustering and Dimensionality Reduction Concepts

Unsupervised learning is a type of machine learning where the algorithm learns from unlabeled data, meaning the input data is not paired with corresponding output labels.[1] The goal is to discover hidden patterns, structures, and relationships within the data. Two primary tasks in unsupervised learning are clustering and dimensionality reduction.

Clustering:

- **Purpose:** Grouping similar data points together based on their inherent characteristics or similarities.
- **Goal:** To partition the data into clusters such that data points within a cluster are more similar to each other than to data points in other clusters.

- **Applications:** Customer segmentation, image segmentation, document clustering, anomaly detection.
- **Key Concepts:**
  - **Similarity/Distance Metrics:** Measures the similarity or dissimilarity between data points (e.g., Euclidean distance, cosine similarity).[2]
  - **Cluster Centroids:** Representative points of each cluster.[3]
  - **Cluster Assignments:** Assigning data points to the closest cluster centroid.[4]

Dimensionality Reduction:

- **Purpose:** Reducing the number of features (dimensions) in a dataset while preserving its essential information.[5]

- **Goal:** To simplify the data, reduce noise, and improve computational efficiency.
- **Applications:** Data visualization, feature extraction, noise reduction, and improving the performance of machine learning algorithms.[6]
- **Key Concepts:**
  - ○ **Feature Extraction:** Creating new features that are combinations of the original features.[7]
  - ○ **Feature Selection:** Selecting a subset of the original features.[8]
  - ○ **Projection:** Projecting the data into a lower-dimensional space.[9]

Why Unsupervised Learning?

- **Unlabeled Data:** Many real-world datasets are unlabeled, making supervised learning inapplicable.[10]
- **Pattern Discovery:** Unsupervised learning can uncover hidden patterns and structures that might not be apparent in labeled data.[11]
- **Data Exploration:** It provides insights into the data's underlying characteristics and relationships.[12]
- **Preprocessing:** Dimensionality reduction can improve the performance of supervised learning algorithms by reducing noise and redundancy.[13]

6.2 K-Means Clustering: Grouping Data into Clusters

K-Means clustering is a popular and widely used unsupervised learning algorithm for partitioning data into k clusters.[14]

Key Concepts:

- **Number of Clusters (k):** A user-defined parameter that specifies the number of clusters to be formed.[15]
- **Centroids:** Representative points of each cluster, initially chosen randomly or using heuristics.
- **Assignment Step:** Assign each data point to the nearest centroid based on a distance metric (e.g., Euclidean distance).
- **Update Step:** Recalculate the centroids as the mean of the data points assigned to each cluster.[16]
- **Iteration:** Repeat the assignment and update steps until the centroids converge or a stopping criterion is met.[17]

K-Means Algorithm:

1. **Initialization:** Choose k initial centroids.

2. **Assignment:** Assign each data point to the nearest centroid.
3. **Update:** Recalculate[18] the centroids as the mean of the data points in each cluster.
4. **Iteration:** Repeat steps 2 and 3 until convergence.[19]

Choosing the Number of Clusters (k):

- **Elbow Method:** Plot the within-cluster sum of squares (WCSS) for different values of k and choose the k at the "elbow" point, where the rate of decrease in WCSS slows down.[20]
- **Silhouette Score:** Measures how similar a data point is to its own cluster compared to other clusters. Higher silhouette scores indicate better clustering.[21]
- **Domain Knowledge:** Use domain knowledge to determine the appropriate number of clusters.

Advantages of K-Means:

- **Simplicity:** Easy to understand and implement.
- **Efficiency:** Relatively efficient for large datasets.
- **Scalability:** Scales well to large datasets.

Disadvantages of K-Means:

- **Sensitivity to Initialization:** The initial choice of centroids can significantly affect the results.[22]
- **Assumption of Spherical Clusters:** Assumes that clusters are spherical and equally sized.[23]
- **Need to Choose k:** Requires the user to specify the number of clusters.
- **Sensitivity to Outliers:** Outliers can significantly affect the centroids.[24]

Applications:

- **Customer Segmentation:** Grouping customers based on purchasing behavior or demographics.[25]
- **Image Segmentation:** Partitioning an image into regions based on pixel values.[26]
- **Document Clustering:** Grouping documents based on their content.
- **Anomaly Detection:** Identifying data points that deviate significantly from the clusters.

6.3 Hierarchical Clustering: Building Dendrograms and Identifying Clusters

Hierarchical clustering is another popular unsupervised learning algorithm that builds a hierarchy of clusters.[27]

Key Concepts:

- **Dendrogram:** A tree-like diagram that represents the hierarchy of clusters.[28]
- **Agglomerative Clustering (Bottom-Up):** Starts with each data point as a separate cluster and iteratively merges the closest clusters.
- **Divisive Clustering (Top-Down):** Starts with all data points in a single cluster and iteratively splits the clusters.
- **Linkage Methods:** Define how the distance between clusters is calculated:
  - **Single Linkage:** Minimum distance between any two points in the clusters.
  - **Complete Linkage:** Maximum distance between any two points in the clusters.
  - **Average Linkage:** Average distance between all pairs of points in the clusters.[29][30]

- ○ **Ward's Method:** Minimizes the variance within clusters.

Hierarchical Clustering Algorithm (Agglomerative):

1. **Initialization:** Start with each data point as a separate cluster.
2. **Distance Matrix:** Calculate the distance matrix between all pairs of clusters.
3. **Merge Clusters:** Merge the two closest clusters based on the linkage method.
4. **Update Distance Matrix:** Update the distance matrix based on the merged clusters.
5. **Repeat:** Repeat steps 3 and 4 until all data points are in a single cluster.

Building Dendrograms:

- Dendrograms visually represent the hierarchy of clusters.[31]
- The height of the branches in the dendrogram indicates the distance between clusters.[32]
- Cutting the dendrogram at a specific height determines the number of clusters.

Identifying Clusters:

- Cut the dendrogram at a specific height to obtain the desired number of clusters.[33]
- The clusters are represented by the branches below the cut.

Advantages of Hierarchical Clustering:

- **Dendrogram Visualization:** Provides a visual representation of the cluster hierarchy.[34]

- **No Need to Specify k:** Does not require the user to specify the number of clusters beforehand.
- **Flexibility:** Can handle different cluster shapes and sizes.

Disadvantages of Hierarchical Clustering:

- **Computational Cost:** Can be computationally expensive for large datasets.[35]
- **Sensitivity to Linkage Method:** The choice of linkage method can significantly affect the results.[36]
- **Difficulty in Handling High-Dimensional Data:** Can be challenging to visualize and interpret dendrograms for high-dimensional data.

Applications:

- **Taxonomy:** Classifying organisms based on their characteristics.[37]
- **Document Clustering:** Grouping documents based on their content hierarchy.
- **Customer Segmentation:** Grouping customers based on their purchasing behavior or demographics.[38]

By understanding the concepts of clustering and dimensionality reduction, particularly K-Means and hierarchical clustering, you can explore and discover hidden patterns in your data, even without labeled outputs.

6.4 Principal Component Analysis (PCA): Reducing Dimensionality

Principal Component Analysis (PCA) is a widely used dimensionality reduction technique that transforms high-dimensional data into a lower-dimensional representation while preserving as much variance as possible.[12]

Key Concepts:

- **Linear Transformation:** PCA performs a linear transformation of the data, projecting it onto a new set of orthogonal axes called principal components.[3]
- **Variance Preservation:** The principal components are ordered by the amount of variance they explain, with the first component explaining the most variance.[45]

- **Orthogonality:** The principal components are orthogonal (uncorrelated), which helps to remove redundancy in the data.[6]
- **Eigenvectors and Eigenvalues:** PCA uses eigenvectors and eigenvalues to determine the principal components.[7] Eigenvectors represent the directions of the principal components, and eigenvalues represent the amount of variance explained by each component.[8]

PCA Algorithm:

1. **Standardize the Data:** Scale the data to have zero mean and unit variance.
2. **Compute the Covariance Matrix:** Calculate the covariance matrix of the standardized data.
3. **Compute[9] Eigenvectors and Eigenvalues:** Calculate the

eigenvectors and eigenvalues of the covariance matrix.[10]

4. **Select Principal Components:** Select the top k eigenvectors based on their eigenvalues, where k is the desired number of dimensions.[11]

5. **Transform the Data:** Project the data onto the selected principal components.

Explained Variance Ratio:

- The explained variance ratio represents the proportion of variance explained by each principal component.[12][13]
- It can be used to determine the number of principal components to retain.
- The sum of the explained variance ratios of the selected components indicates the total variance preserved in the reduced-dimensional data.

Advantages of PCA:

- **Dimensionality Reduction:** Reduces the number of features, simplifying the data and improving computational efficiency.[14]
- **Noise Reduction:** Can help to reduce noise in the data.[15]
- **Data Visualization:** Projects high-dimensional data into a lower-dimensional space for visualization.[16]
- **Feature Extraction:** Creates new features that are linear combinations of the original features.[17]

Disadvantages of PCA:

- **Linearity Assumption:** Assumes that the data can be represented by linear combinations of the original features.[18]

- **Sensitivity to Scaling:** Feature scaling is crucial for PCA to perform well.
- **Loss of Information:** Dimensionality reduction inevitably leads to some loss of information.
- **Interpretability:** The principal components may not be easily interpretable in terms of the original features.

Applications:

- **Image Compression:** Reducing the number of pixels in an image.[19]
- **Face Recognition:** Extracting features from facial images.[20]
- **Genomics:** Analyzing gene expression data.[21]
- **Financial Data Analysis:** Identifying patterns in stock market data.[22]

6.5 t-Distributed Stochastic Neighbor Embedding (t-SNE): Visualizing High-Dimensional Data

t-Distributed Stochastic Neighbor Embedding (t-SNE) is a non-linear dimensionality reduction technique primarily used for visualizing high-dimensional data[23] in a low-dimensional space (typically 2D or 3D).[24]

Key Concepts:

- **Non-Linear Dimensionality Reduction:** t-SNE can handle complex, non-linear relationships in the data.[25]
- **Probability Distributions:** t-SNE models the similarity between data points in the high-dimensional space

and the low-dimensional space using probability distributions.

- **Joint Probabilities:** In the high-dimensional space, t-SNE computes the joint probabilities of data points being neighbors based on Gaussian distributions.[26]

- **t-Distribution:** In the low-dimensional space, t-SNE computes the joint probabilities of data points being neighbors based on t-distributions.[27]

- **Minimizing Divergence:** t-SNE minimizes the divergence between the probability distributions in the high-dimensional and low-dimensional spaces using gradient descent.[28]

t-SNE Algorithm:

1. **Compute Pairwise Similarities:** Calculate the pairwise similarities between data points in the

high-dimensional space using Gaussian distributions.

2. **Compute Joint Probabilities:** Calculate the joint probabilities of data points being neighbors in the high-dimensional space.

3. **Initialize Low-Dimensional Embeddings:** Initialize the low-dimensional embeddings of the data points randomly.

4. **Compute Pairwise Similarities in Low-Dimensional Space:** Calculate the pairwise similarities between data points in the low-dimensional space using t-distributions.

5. **Compute Joint Probabilities in Low-Dimensional Space:** Calculate the joint probabilities of data points being neighbors in the low-dimensional space.

6. **Minimize Divergence:** Minimize the Kullback-Leibler (KL) divergence between the probability distributions in the high-dimensional and

low-dimensional spaces[29] using gradient descent.

7. **Iterate:** Repeat steps 4-6 until convergence.

Advantages of t-SNE:

- **Visualizing Non-Linear Data:** Can effectively visualize complex, non-linear relationships in the data.
- **Preserving Local Structure:** Tends to preserve the local structure of the data, meaning that nearby points in the high-dimensional space are also nearby in the low-dimensional space.[30]
- **Revealing Clusters:** Can reveal clusters and patterns that might not be apparent in other dimensionality reduction techniques.[31]

Disadvantages of t-SNE:

- **Computational Cost:** Can be computationally expensive, especially for large datasets.[32]
- **Sensitivity to Hyperparameters:** The results can be sensitive to the choice of hyperparameters, such as perplexity and learning rate.
- **Global Structure Loss:** Tends to lose the global structure of the data, meaning that the distances between clusters in the low-dimensional space may not accurately reflect the distances in the high-dimensional space.
- **Non-Deterministic:** The results can vary slightly depending on the random initialization.
- **Not for Dimensionality Reduction for Machine Learning:** t-SNE is primarily for visualization, and the transformed data is not well suited for use in other machine learning algorithms.

Applications:

- **Visualizing High-Dimensional Datasets:** Visualizing complex datasets with many features.
- **Exploring Data Structures:** Discovering clusters and patterns in the data.
- **Analyzing Biological Data:** Visualizing gene expression data or protein structures.[33]
- **Natural Language Processing (NLP):** Visualizing word embeddings.

By understanding PCA and t-SNE, you can effectively reduce the dimensionality of your data and visualize complex patterns, enabling you to gain valuable insights from your datasets.

CHAPTER 7

Neural Networks and Deep Learning Fundamentals

Neural networks, inspired by the brain, are composed of interconnected neurons organized in layers.[1] Deep learning utilizes multi-layered neural networks to learn complex patterns from data.[2] Key concepts include weights, biases, activation functions, forward and backward propagation, loss functions, and optimization algorithms.[3] Frameworks like TensorFlow/Keras simplify building and training these models, enabling applications in diverse fields like image recognition and natural language processing.[4]

7.1 Introduction to Neural Networks: Architecture and Concepts

Neural networks, inspired by the structure and function of the human brain, are a powerful class of machine learning models capable of learning complex patterns from data.[1] They form the foundation of deep learning, a subfield of machine learning that has revolutionized various domains.[2]

Key Concepts:

- **Neurons (Nodes):** The basic building blocks of neural networks.[3] Each neuron receives input signals, processes them, and produces an output signal.[4]
- **Weights:** Numerical values associated with the connections between neurons, representing the strength of the connections.[5]

- **Biases:** Numerical values added to the weighted sum of inputs, allowing the neuron to shift its activation function.[6]
- **Activation Functions:** Non-linear functions applied to the weighted sum of inputs and biases, introducing non-linearity into the network.[7] Common activation functions include:
  - **Sigmoid:** Maps inputs to a range between 0 and 1.
  - **ReLU (Rectified Linear Unit):** Outputs the input directly if it is positive, otherwise outputs zero.[8]
  - **Tanh (Hyperbolic Tangent):** Maps inputs to a range between -1 and 1.[9]
  - **Softmax:** Converts a vector of real numbers into a probability distribution.[10]
-
- **Layers:** Neurons are organized into layers, including:

- ○ **Input Layer:** Receives the input data.[11]
- ○ **Hidden Layers:** Intermediate layers that perform feature extraction and transformation.[12]
- ○ **Output Layer:** Produces the final output of the network.[13]
- **Feedforward Neural Networks (FNNs):** Information flows in one direction, from the input layer to the output layer, without any loops or cycles.[14]
- **Deep Neural Networks (DNNs):** Neural networks with multiple hidden layers.[15]
- **Forward Propagation:** The process of computing the output of the network by propagating input signals through the layers.[16]
- **Backward Propagation (Backpropagation):** The process of computing the gradients of the loss function with respect to the weights

and biases, used to update the network's parameters.[17]

- **Loss Function:** A function that measures the error between the predicted output and the actual output.[18]
- **Optimization Algorithms:** Algorithms used to update the network's parameters to minimize the loss function, such as:
  - **Gradient Descent:** Iteratively updates the parameters in the direction of the negative gradient.
  - **Adam (Adaptive Moment Estimation):** An adaptive learning rate optimization algorithm.

Architecture of a Neural Network:

- A typical feedforward neural network consists of an input layer, one or more hidden layers, and an output layer.[19]
- Each neuron in a layer is connected to all neurons in the[20] next layer.[21]
- The connections between neurons are associated with weights and biases.[22]
- The output of each neuron is computed by applying an activation function to the weighted sum of its inputs and biases.

7.2 Building Simple Neural Networks with TensorFlow/Keras

TensorFlow and Keras are popular deep learning frameworks that provide tools and libraries for building and training neural networks.[23]

TensorFlow:

- A powerful open-source machine learning framework developed by Google.[24]
- Provides a comprehensive set of tools and libraries for building and deploying deep learning models.[25]
- Supports both low-level and high-level APIs.[26]

Keras:

- A high-level neural networks API that runs on top of TensorFlow.[27]
- Provides a user-friendly interface for building and training neural networks.[28]
- Simplifies the process of creating complex deep learning models.

Building a Simple Neural Network with Keras:

1. **Import Libraries:**

2. Python

import tensorflow as tf
from tensorflow import keras

3.
4.
5. **Define the Model:**
6. Python

```
model = keras.Sequential([
    keras.layers.Dense(128, activation='relu', input_shape=(input_dim,)),
                    keras.layers.Dense(10, activation='softmax') #example of 10 output classes
])
```

7.

- keras.Sequential: Creates a sequential model, where layers are added one after another.
- keras.layers.Dense: Creates a fully connected layer.
- input_shape: Specifies the shape of the input data.
- activation: Specifies the activation function.

8. **Compile the Model:**
9. Python

```
model.compile(optimizer='adam',
    loss='categorical_crossentropy',
    metrics=['accuracy'])
```

10.

- optimizer: Specifies the optimization algorithm.
- loss: Specifies the loss function.
- metrics: Specifies the metrics to be evaluated.

11. **Train the Model:**

12. Python

```python
model.fit(X_train, y_train, epochs=10, batch_size=32)
```

13.
- o X_train: Training data.
- o y_train: Training labels.
- o epochs: The number of times the model iterates over the training data.
- o batch_size: The number of samples processed in each batch.

14. **Evaluate the Model:**

15. Python

```python
loss, accuracy = model.evaluate(X_test, y_test)
print(f"Loss: {loss}, Accuracy: {accuracy}")
```

16.

   o X_test: Test data.
   o y_test: Test labels.

Key Considerations:

- **Data Preprocessing:** Preprocessing the data, such as scaling and normalization, is crucial for training neural networks.[29]
- **Hyperparameter Tuning:** Tuning the hyperparameters, such as the number of layers, the number of neurons, and the learning rate, can significantly impact model performance.[30]
- **Overfitting:** Neural networks are prone to overfitting, especially with complex models and small datasets.[31] Techniques like regularization and dropout can help to prevent overfitting.[32]

- **Computational   Resources:** Training deep neural networks can require significant computational resources, such as GPUs.[33]

By understanding the architecture and concepts of neural networks and using TensorFlow/Keras, you can build and train powerful deep learning models for a wide range of applications.

7.3 Activation Functions, Loss Functions, and Optimization Algorithms

These three components are fundamental to the training and performance of neural networks.

Activation Functions:

- **Purpose:** Introduce non-linearity into the network, enabling it to learn complex patterns.[1] Without non-linear activation functions, a neural network would simply be a linear regression model.[2]

- **Types:**
  - **Sigmoid (Logistic):**
    - Formula: $\sigma(z) = 1 / (1 + e^{(-z)})$[3]
    - Output range: $(0, 1)$[4]
    - Use case: Binary classification (output as probability).
    - Drawbacks: Vanishing gradients, not zero-centered.[5]
  - **Tanh (Hyperbolic Tangent):**[6]
    - Formula: $\tanh(z) = (e^{z} - e^{(-z)}) / (e^{z} + e^{(-z)})$[7]
    - Output range: $(-1, 1)$[8]
    - Use case: Hidden layers.
    - Drawbacks: Vanishing gradients.
  -

- **ReLU (Rectified Linear Unit):**[9]
  - Formula: $\text{ReLU}(z) = \max(0, z)$[10]
  - Output range: $[0, \infty)$
  - Use case: Hidden layers.
  - Advantages: Computationally efficient, mitigates vanishing gradients.
  - Drawbacks: Dying ReLU problem (neurons can become inactive).[11]
-
- **Leaky ReLU:**
  - Formula: $\text{LeakyReLU}(z) = \max(\alpha z, z)$ (where α is a small constant)
  - Use case: Hidden layers (addresses dying ReLU).
- **Softmax:**
  - Formula: $\text{Softmax}(z)\_i = e^{\wedge}(z\_i) / \Sigma e^{\wedge}(z\_j)$[12]

- Output range: Probability distribution over classes.
- Use case: Multiclass classification (output layer).

Loss Functions:

- **Purpose:** Quantify the error between the predicted output and the actual output, guiding the optimization process.
- **Types:**
  - **Mean Squared Error (MSE):**
    - Use case: Regression.
    - Formula: MSE = $(1/n)$ $\Sigma(y\_true - y\_pred)^2$
  - **Binary Cross-Entropy:**
    - Use case: Binary classification.

- Formula: $-[y\_true * \log(y\_pred) + (1 - y\_true) * \log(1 - y\_pred)]$
- **Categorical Cross-Entropy:**
  - Use case: Multiclass classification.
  - Formula: $-\Sigma(y\_true * \log(y\_pred))$
- **Sparse Categorical Cross-Entropy:**
  - Use case: Multiclass classification when labels are integers.
  - Useful when dealing with very large amounts of classes.
- **Hinge Loss:**
  - Use case: Support Vector Machines (SVMs) and some classification problems.

Optimization Algorithms:

- **Purpose:** Update the network's weights and biases to minimize the loss function.
- **Types:**
  - **Gradient Descent:**
    - Iteratively updates parameters in the direction of the negative gradient.
    - Variants: Batch gradient descent, stochastic gradient descent (SGD), mini-batch gradient descent.[13]
  - **Adam (Adaptive Moment Estimation):**
    - Combines the benefits of AdaGrad and RMSProp.[14]
    - Adaptive learning rates for each parameter.
    - Widely used and effective.

- ○ **RMSProp (Root Mean Square Propagation):**
  - Adapts the learning rate based on the magnitude of recent gradients.[15]
- ○ **AdaGrad (Adaptive Gradient Algorithm):**
  - Adapts the learning rate based on the historical sum of squared gradients.

7.4 Training Neural Networks: Backpropagation and Gradient Descent

Backpropagation and gradient descent are the core algorithms used to train neural networks.[16]

Backpropagation:

- **Purpose:** Calculate the gradients of the loss function with respect to the network's weights and biases.
- **Process:**
    1. **Forward Pass:** Compute the network's output and loss.
    2. **Backward Pass:** Propagate the error gradients from the output layer to the input layer, using the chain rule of calculus.[17]
    3. **Weight and Bias Updates:** Update the weights and biases using the calculated gradients and an optimization algorithm.

Gradient Descent:

- **Purpose:** Minimize the loss function by iteratively updating the network's parameters.
- **Process:**
    1. **Calculate Gradients:** Compute the gradients of the

loss function with respect to the parameters.

2. **Update Parameters:** Update the parameters in the direction of the negative gradient, scaled by a learning rate.
3. **Repeat:** Repeat steps 1 and 2 until convergence.

Training Process:

1. **Data Preprocessing:** Prepare the data for training (e.g., scaling, normalization).
2. **Model Initialization:** Initialize the network's weights and biases.
3. **Forward Propagation:** Compute the network's output and loss.
4. **Backward Propagation:** Calculate the gradients of the loss function.
5. **Parameter Updates:** Update the network's parameters using an optimization algorithm.

6. **Iteration:** Repeat steps 3-5 for a specified number of epochs.
7. **Evaluation:** Evaluate the model's performance on a validation set.

7.5 Introduction to Convolutional Neural Networks (CNNs) and Recurrent Neural Networks (RNNs)

CNNs and RNNs are specialized neural network architectures designed for specific types of data.[18]

Convolutional Neural Networks (CNNs):

- **Purpose:** Process and analyze grid-like data, such as images and videos.
- **Key Concepts:**
  - **Convolutional Layers:** Extract features by applying

filters (kernels) to the input data.[19]

- ○ **Pooling Layers:** Reduce the spatial dimensions of the feature maps, reducing computational cost.[20]
- ○ **Activation Functions:** Introduce non-linearity.
- ○ **Fully Connected Layers:** Perform classification or regression.
- **Applications:** Image classification, object detection, image segmentation, facial recognition.

Recurrent Neural Networks (RNNs):

- **Purpose:** Process and analyze sequential data, such as text, audio, and time series.
- **Key Concepts:**
  - ○ **Recurrent Connections:** Allow the network to maintain a memory of past inputs.[21]

- ○ **Hidden States:** Store the network's memory.
- ○ **Backpropagation Through Time (BPTT):** An algorithm for training RNNs.
- ○ **LSTM (Long Short-Term Memory) and GRU (Gated Recurrent Unit):** Variants of RNNs that address the vanishing gradient problem.[22]
- **Applications:** Natural language processing (NLP), speech recognition, machine translation, time series forecasting.

CNN vs RNN:

- **CNNs:** Excellent for spatial data.[23]
- **RNNs:** Excellent for sequential data.[24]
- **Hybrid Models:** Combining CNNs and RNNs can be effective for tasks involving both spatial and sequential data (e.g., video analysis).

By understanding these fundamental concepts and architectures, you can build and train powerful neural networks for a wide range of applications.

Part III:

Practical Applications and Advanced Topics

CHAPTER 8

Natural Language Processing (NLP) with Python

NLP empowers computers to understand and process human language. Python, with libraries like NLTK, spaCy, and Transformers, offers tools for tasks like text preprocessing (tokenization, stemming, lemmatization), text representation (Bag of Words, TF-IDF, word embeddings), sentiment analysis, and machine translation. These techniques enable applications like chatbots, text summarization, and information retrieval, bridging the gap between human communication and machine understanding.

8.1 Text Preprocessing: Tokenization, Stemming, and Lemmatization

Text preprocessing is a crucial step in NLP, preparing raw text data for analysis and modeling.[1] It involves cleaning, normalizing, and transforming text into a format suitable for machine learning algorithms.[2]

1. Tokenization:

- **Purpose:** Breaking down text into individual words, phrases, symbols, or other meaningful elements called tokens.[3]
- **Methods:**
  - **Word Tokenization:** Splitting text into individual words.[4]
  - **Sentence Tokenization:** Splitting text into individual sentences.[5]

- o **Subword Tokenization:** Splitting words into smaller units (e.g., characters, subwords).[6]
- **Tools:**
  - o nltk.tokenize (Natural Language Toolkit): Provides various tokenization methods.
  - o spaCy: Offers efficient and accurate tokenization.
  - o Transformers library from Huggingface: provides tokenizer classes for many state of the art models.
- **Considerations:** Handling punctuation, special characters, and contractions.[7]

2. Stemming:

- **Purpose:** Reducing words to their root or base form by removing suffixes and prefixes.[8]
- **Methods:**

- ○ **Porter Stemmer:** A widely used stemming algorithm.[9]
- ○ **Snowball Stemmer:** An improved version of the Porter Stemmer.[10]
- **Tools:**
  - ○ nltk.stem.PorterStemmer
  - ○ nltk.stem.SnowballStemmer
- **Drawbacks:**
  - ○ Can produce non-words (e.g., "comput" from "computing").[11]
  - ○ May over-stem or under-stem words.
  - ○ Less accurate than lemmatization.[12]

3. Lemmatization:

- **Purpose:** Reducing words to their base or dictionary form (lemma) by considering the word's meaning and context.[13]

- **Methods:**
  - Using a vocabulary and morphological analysis to find the lemma.
- **Tools:**
  - nltk.stem.WordNetLemmatizer (requires WordNet lexical database).
  - spaCy: Provides accurate lemmatization.
- **Advantages:**
  - Produces valid words.
  - More accurate than stemming.
- **Drawbacks:**
  - Computationally more expensive than stemming.[14]

Other Text Preprocessing Steps:

- **Lowercasing:** Converting all text to lowercase.

- **Removing Stop Words:** Removing common words that don't carry much meaning (e.g., "the," "a," "is").[15]
- **Removing Punctuation and Special Characters:** Cleaning the text from unwanted symbols.[16]
- **Handling Numbers:** Removing or converting numbers.
- **Correcting Spelling Errors:** Using spell-checking tools.
- **Expanding Contractions:** Converting contractions to their full forms (e.g., "can't" to "cannot").

8.2 Text Representation: Bag of Words, TF-IDF, and Word Embeddings

Text representation is the process of converting text data into numerical vectors that can be used as input for machine learning algorithms.[17][18]

1. Bag of Words (BoW):

- **Purpose:** Representing text as a collection of words and their frequencies, ignoring word order and grammar.
- **Process:**
    - Create a vocabulary of all unique words in the corpus.
    - For each document, create a vector where each element represents the frequency of a word in the vocabulary.
- **Advantages:**
    - Simple and easy to implement.
    - Effective for some text classification tasks.
- **Disadvantages:**
    - Ignores word order and grammar.
    - Creates high-dimensional and sparse vectors.
    - Doesn't capture semantic relationships between words.

2. Term Frequency-Inverse Document Frequency (TF-IDF):

- **Purpose:** Representing text by considering the importance of words in a document relative to the entire corpus.
- **Components:**
  - **Term Frequency (TF):** Measures how often a word appears in a document.[19]
  - **Inverse Document Frequency (IDF):** Measures how rare a word is in the corpus.[20]
- **Formula:** TF-IDF = TF * IDF
- **Advantages:**
  - Weights words based on their importance.
  - Reduces the impact of common words.
- **Disadvantages:**
  - Ignores word order and grammar.

- ○ Creates high-dimensional and sparse vectors.
  - ○ Doesn't capture semantic relationships between words.
- **Implementation:** Scikit-learn's TfidfVectorizer class.

3. Word Embeddings:

- **Purpose:** Representing words as dense, low-dimensional vectors that capture semantic relationships between words.
- **Methods:**
  - ○ **Word2Vec:** Learns word embeddings by predicting neighboring words.
  - ○ **GloVe (Global Vectors for Word Representation):** Learns word embeddings by factorizing a word-context matrix.

- FastText: Learns word embeddings by considering subword information.[21]
- **Transformer-based Embeddings (BERT, RoBERTa, etc.):** Contextualized word embeddings that capture complex semantic relationships.[22]

- **Advantages:**
  - Captures semantic relationships between words.
  - Creates dense and low-dimensional vectors.
  - Improves the performance of many NLP tasks.

- **Disadvantages:**
  - Requires large amounts of training data.
  - Can be computationally expensive to train.

- **Implementation:**

- Gensim library (Word2Vec, GloVe).
- Transformers library (BERT, RoBERTa, etc.).[23]

Key Considerations for Text Representation:

- **Vocabulary Size:** Limiting the vocabulary size can reduce the dimensionality of the vectors.
- **N-grams:** Considering sequences of n words (n-grams) can capture some word order information.[24]
- **Contextual Embeddings:** Using contextual embeddings (e.g., BERT) can capture complex semantic relationships.[25]
- **Domain-Specific Embeddings:** Training embeddings on domain-specific data can improve performance for specific tasks.[26]

By mastering text preprocessing and representation techniques, you can effectively transform raw text data into a format suitable for building powerful NLP applications.

8.3 Sentiment Analysis: Building Models to Analyze Textual Sentiment

Sentiment analysis is a crucial NLP task that aims to determine the emotional tone or sentiment expressed in text.[1] It has wide-ranging applications in understanding customer feedback, social media monitoring, and market research.[2]

Key Concepts:

- **Sentiment Polarity:** The overall sentiment expressed in text, typically categorized as positive, negative, or neutral.[3]

- **Sentiment Intensity:** The strength or degree of the sentiment.
- **Subjectivity vs. Objectivity:** Distinguishing between subjective opinions and objective facts.
- **Aspect-Based Sentiment Analysis:** Identifying sentiment towards specific aspects or features of a product or service.[4]

Methods for Sentiment Analysis:

- **Lexicon-Based Approaches:**
  - Using predefined dictionaries or lexicons of words and their associated sentiment scores.[5]
  - Calculating the overall sentiment by aggregating the scores of individual words.
  - Examples: VADER (Valence Aware Dictionary and sEntiment Reasoner), TextBlob.[6]
  - Advantages: Simple, fast, and easy to implement.[7]

- Disadvantages: Limited to the words in the lexicon, may not capture context or nuances.[8]
- **Machine Learning Approaches:**
  - Training machine learning models on labeled datasets of text and their corresponding sentiment labels.[9]
  - Using features like bag-of-words, TF-IDF, or word embeddings.[10]
  - Common algorithms: Naive Bayes, Support Vector Machines (SVMs), Logistic Regression, and deep learning models (e.g., RNNs, Transformers).[11]
  - Advantages: Can capture complex patterns and context, adaptable to different domains.[12]
  - Disadvantages: Requires labeled training data, can be computationally expensive.
- **Deep Learning Approaches:**

- Utilizing Recurrent Neural Networks (RNNs), Convolutional Neural Networks (CNNs), and Transformer models (BERT, RoBERTa, etc.) to learn contextualized representations of text and capture complex sentiment patterns.[13]
- These models often achieve state-of-the-art performance in sentiment analysis tasks.[14]
- Advantages: Capture complex contextual relationships, high accuracy.
- Disadvantages: Require large datasets, computationally expensive, and can be harder to interpret.

Evaluation Metrics:

- **Accuracy:** The proportion of correctly classified sentiment labels.
- **Precision:** The proportion of correctly predicted positive sentiments out of all predicted positive sentiments.
- **Recall:** The proportion of correctly predicted positive sentiments out of all actual positive sentiments.
- **F1-score:** The harmonic mean of precision and recall.
- **Confusion Matrix:** A table that shows the number of correctly and incorrectly classified sentiment labels.[15]

8.4 Topic Modeling: Discovering Latent Topics in Text Data

Topic modeling is an unsupervised learning technique that aims to discover hidden or latent topics in a collection of documents.[16]

It helps to understand the main themes and patterns in large text corpora.

Key Concepts:

- **Latent Topics:** Hidden themes or concepts that are present in the documents.[17]
- **Topic Distributions:** The probability distribution of topics in each document.
- **Word Distributions:** The probability distribution of words in each topic.

Methods for Topic Modeling:

- **Latent Dirichlet Allocation (LDA):**
  - A probabilistic model that assumes documents are mixtures of topics and topics are mixtures of words.

- Uses Bayesian inference to estimate the topic and word distributions.
- Implementation: Gensim library.
- Advantages: Effective for discovering coherent topics, widely used.
- Disadvantages: Requires tuning hyperparameters, can be sensitive to data preprocessing.

- **Non-Negative Matrix Factorization (NMF):**
  - A matrix factorization technique that decomposes the document-term matrix into two non-negative matrices: document-topic and topic-term.
  - Implementation: Scikit-learn.
  - Advantages: Can produce interpretable topics, computationally efficient.
  - Disadvantages: Can be sensitive to initialization.

- **Top2Vec:**
  - An algorithm that learns jointly embedded topic, document, and word vectors.
  - Uses Doc2Vec and dimensionality reduction techniques.[18]
  - Advantages: Fast, robust, and produces coherent topics.
  - Disadvantages: Less control over the topic discovery process.

Evaluation Metrics:

- **Topic Coherence:** Measures the semantic similarity between the words in a topic.
- **Perplexity:** Measures how well a topic model predicts a sample.[19] Lower perplexity indicates better performance.

- **Visualizations:** Using tools like pyLDAvis to visualize the topics and their relationships.[20]

8.5 Applications of NLP: Chatbots, Text Summarization, and More

NLP has a wide range of applications in various domains, including:

- **Chatbots:**
  - Developing conversational agents that can interact with users in natural language.
  - Using techniques like intent recognition, entity extraction, and dialogue management.
  - Applications: Customer support, virtual assistants, and information retrieval.
- **Text Summarization:**

- Generating concise summaries of long documents or articles.
- Methods: Extractive summarization (selecting key sentences) and abstractive summarization (generating new sentences).[21]
- Applications: News summarization, document analysis, and content generation.

- **Machine Translation:**
  - Translating text from one language to another.
  - Using deep learning models like sequence-to-sequence models and Transformers.[22]
  - Applications: Global communication, localization, and multilingual content.[23]

- **Information Retrieval:**
  - Retrieving relevant information from large text corpora.

- Using techniques like keyword search, semantic search, and question answering.
- Applications: Search engines, document retrieval systems, and knowledge bases.
- **Named Entity Recognition (NER):**
  - Identifying and classifying named entities (e.g., people, organizations, locations) in text.
  - Applications: Information extraction, knowledge graph construction, and question answering.
- **Part-of-Speech (POS) Tagging:**
  - Assigning grammatical tags (e.g., nouns, verbs, adjectives) to words in a sentence.
  - Applications: Syntactic analysis, text generation, and information extraction.
- **Text Classification:**

- Categorizing text into predefined classes or categories.
- Applications: Spam detection, sentiment analysis, and topic classification.

- **Question Answering:**
  - Building systems that can answer questions posed in natural language.
  - Applications: Virtual assistants, chatbots, and search engines.[24]

- **Text Generation:**
  - Generating human-like text using language models.
  - Applications: Content generation, creative writing, and dialogue systems.

By mastering sentiment analysis, topic modeling, and the diverse applications of NLP, you can unlock the power of language data and build intelligent systems that understand and interact with humans in a natural way.

CHAPTER 9

Computer Vision with Python

Python, with libraries like OpenCV and Pillow, enables powerful computer vision applications. Image processing basics include reading, manipulating, and displaying images. Feature extraction techniques like edge and corner detection, along with feature descriptors (SIFT, ORB), facilitate object recognition and image analysis. These tools empower tasks such as image classification, object detection, and image segmentation, bridging the gap between digital images and intelligent interpretation.

9.1 Image Processing Basics: Reading, Manipulating, and Displaying Images

Image processing is the foundation of computer vision, involving the manipulation and analysis of digital images.[1] Python, with libraries like OpenCV and Pillow, provides powerful tools for these tasks.[2]

1. Reading Images:

- **OpenCV (cv2):**
    - A powerful library for computer vision and image processing.[3]
    - Reads images as NumPy arrays.
    - Supports various image formats (e.g., JPEG, PNG, BMP).[4]
    - cv2.imread(): Reads an image from a file.
    - Example:
    - Python

```
import cv2
image = cv2.imread('image.jpg')
```

    ○

    ○

- **Pillow (PIL):**
  - A Python Imaging Library that provides image processing capabilities.[5]
  - Reads images as PIL Image objects.[6]
  - Supports various image formats.[7]
  - Image.open(): Opens an image file.
  - Example:
  - Python

```
from PIL import Image
image = Image.open('image.jpg')
```

- ○
  - ○

2. Displaying Images:

- **OpenCV:**
  - ○ cv2.imshow(): Displays an image in a window.
  - ○ cv2.waitKey(): Waits for a key event.
  - ○ cv2.destroyAllWindows(): Closes all image windows.
  - ○ Example:
  - ○ Python

```
cv2.imshow('Image', image)
cv2.waitKey(0)
cv2.destroyAllWindows()
```

- o
- o

- **Matplotlib:**
  - o matplotlib.pyplot.imshow(): Displays an image.
  - o Example:
  - o Python

```
import matplotlib.pyplot as plt
plt.imshow(cv2.cvtColor(image,
cv2.COLOR_BGR2RGB))   #Convert   from
BGR to RGB if using cv2
plt.show()
```

- o
- o

- **Pillow:**
  - o image.show(): Displays an image using the default image viewer.

3. Image Manipulation:

- **Resizing:**
  - cv2.resize(): Resizes an image.
  - PIL.Image.resize(): Resizes an image.
- **Cropping:**
  - NumPy array slicing (OpenCV): cropped_image = image[y1:y2, x1:x2]
  - PIL.Image.crop(): Crops an image.
- **Rotating:**
  - cv2.rotate(): Rotates an image.
  - PIL.Image.rotate(): Rotates an image.
- **Flipping:**
  - cv2.flip(): Flips an image horizontally or vertically.
  - PIL.Image.transpose(): Flips or transposes an image.
- **Color Space Conversion:**
  - cv2.cvtColor(): Converts an image from one color space to

another (e.g., BGR to RGB, BGR to grayscale).

- ○ PIL.Image.convert(): Converts an image to a different mode (e.g., RGB to grayscale).
- **Image Blurring:**
  - ○ cv2.GaussianBlur(): Applies a Gaussian blur to an image.
  - ○ cv2.blur(): Applies a simple blur to an image.
- **Image Thresholding:**
  - ○ cv2.threshold(): Applies a threshold to an image, converting it to binary.
  - ○ cv2.adaptiveThreshold(): Applies an adaptive threshold to an image.
- **Drawing Shapes:**
  - ○ cv2.line(), cv2.rectangle(), cv2.circle(), cv2.putText(): Draw lines, rectangles, circles, and text on an image.

9.2 Feature Extraction: Edge Detection, Corner Detection, and Feature Descriptors

Feature extraction is a crucial step in computer vision, involving the identification and extraction of meaningful features from images.

1. Edge Detection:

- **Purpose:** Identifying the boundaries between objects in an image.
- **Methods:**
    - **Sobel Operator:** Calculates the gradient of the image to detect edges.
    - **Canny Edge Detection:** A multi-stage edge detection algorithm that is robust to noise.[8]
    - cv2.Canny(): Applies Canny edge detection.

- **Applications:** Object detection, image segmentation, and shape analysis.

2. Corner Detection:

- **Purpose:** Identifying corner points in an image, which are useful for object recognition and tracking.[9]
- **Methods:**
  - **Harris Corner Detection:** Detects corners based on the local structure of the image.[10]
  - **Shi-Tomasi Corner Detection:** An improved version of the Harris corner detector.[11]
  - cv2.cornerHarris(): Applies Harris corner detection.
  - cv2.goodFeaturesToTrack(): Applies Shi-Tomasi corner detection.
- **Applications:** Object tracking, image stitching, and 3D reconstruction.

3. Feature Descriptors:

- **Purpose:** Representing image features in a compact and informative way, enabling feature matching and object recognition.[12]
- **Types:**
  - **SIFT (Scale-Invariant Feature Transform):**
    - Detects and describes local features that are invariant to scale and rotation.
    - cv2.SIFT_create(): Creates a SIFT object.
  - **SURF (Speeded Up Robust Features):**
    - A faster version of SIFT.
    - cv2.SURF_create(): Creates a SURF object.
  - **ORB (Oriented FAST and Rotated BRIEF):**
    - A fast and efficient feature descriptor that is robust to rotation and scale.

- cv2.ORB_create(): Creates an ORB object.
  - **BRIEF (Binary Robust Independent Elementary Features):**
    - A fast binary descriptor.
    - Used in combination with feature detectors like FAST.
  - **FREAK (Fast Retina Keypoint):**
    - A binary descriptor that is robust to noise and blur.
- **Feature Matching:**
  - Matching features between two images using distance metrics (e.g., Hamming distance, Euclidean distance).
  - cv2.BFMatcher(): Brute-force matcher.
  - cv2.FlannBasedMatcher(): FLANN-based matcher.
- **Applications:** Object recognition, image stitching, and image retrieval.

Key Considerations:

- **Image Preprocessing:** Preprocessing the image, such as noise reduction and color space conversion, can improve the performance of feature extraction algorithms.[13]
- **Feature Selection:** Selecting relevant features can improve the accuracy and efficiency of computer vision tasks.[14]
- **Feature Matching:** Choosing the appropriate feature matching algorithm and distance metric is crucial for accurate feature matching.

By understanding image processing basics and mastering feature extraction techniques, you can build powerful computer vision applications that solve a wide range of real-world problems.

9.3 Convolutional Neural Networks (CNNs) for Image Classification

Convolutional Neural Networks (CNNs) are a specialized type of neural network designed for processing grid-like data, such as images.[1] They have revolutionized image classification tasks, achieving state-of-the-art performance.[2]

Key Concepts:

- **Convolutional Layers:**
    - Apply filters (kernels) to the input image to extract features.[3]
    - Filters slide across the image, computing dot products with local regions.[4]
    - Feature maps are generated, representing the presence of specific features.[5]
- **Pooling Layers:**

- Reduce the spatial dimensions of feature maps, reducing computational cost and making the network more robust to small variations.[6]
- Common pooling operations: Max pooling, average pooling.[7]

- **Activation Functions:**
  - Introduce non-linearity into the network, enabling it to learn complex patterns.[8]
  - ReLU (Rectified Linear Unit) is commonly used in CNNs.[9]

- **Fully Connected Layers:**
  - Perform classification or regression by connecting all neurons in one layer to all neurons in the next layer.[10]
  - Softmax activation is typically used in the output layer for multiclass classification.[11]

- **Architecture:**
  - A typical CNN consists of a series of convolutional and

pooling layers, followed by fully connected layers.[12]

Building CNNs for Image Classification:

1. **Data Preprocessing:**
   - Load and preprocess the image dataset (e.g., resizing, normalization).[13]
   - Split the dataset into training, validation, and test sets.
2. **Model Architecture:**
   - Define the CNN architecture using a deep learning framework like TensorFlow/Keras or PyTorch.
   - Specify the number and types of layers, activation functions, and pooling operations.[14]
3. **Compilation:**

- Compile the model by specifying the loss function, optimizer, and metrics.

4. **Training:**
   - Train the model on the training data using backpropagation and gradient descent.[15]
   - Monitor the model's performance on the validation set to prevent overfitting.

5. **Evaluation:**
   - Evaluate the trained model on the test set to assess its generalization performance.

Transfer Learning:

- Using pre-trained CNN models (e.g., VGG, ResNet, Inception) as feature extractors or fine-tuning them on a new dataset.[16]

- Can significantly improve performance, especially with limited training data.

9.4 Object Detection and Image Segmentation

Object detection and image segmentation are more advanced computer vision tasks that involve identifying and localizing objects in images.[17]

Object Detection:

- **Purpose:** Identifying the presence and location of objects in an image.
- **Methods:**
  - **Region-Based CNNs (R-CNNs):**
    - Generate region proposals and classify them using a CNN.

- Examples: R-CNN, Fast R-CNN, Faster R-CNN.[18]
  - **Single Shot Detectors (SSDs):**
    - Detect objects in a single pass using a convolutional network.[19]
    - Examples: SSD, YOLO (You Only Look Once).
  - **YOLO (You Only Look Once):**
    - Very fast object detection algorithm that predicts bounding boxes and class probabilities in a single forward pass.
- **Key Concepts:**
  - **Bounding Boxes:** Rectangular regions that enclose objects.[20]
  - **Intersection over Union (IoU):** A metric used to evaluate the overlap between predicted and ground-truth bounding boxes.

- **Non-Maximum Suppression (NMS):** A technique used to remove redundant bounding boxes.

Image Segmentation:

- **Purpose:** Partitioning an image into meaningful regions or segments.
- **Types:**
  - **Semantic Segmentation:** Assigning a class label to each pixel in an image.[21]
  - **Instance Segmentation:** Detecting and segmenting individual objects in an image.[22]
- **Methods:**
  - **Fully Convolutional Networks (FCNs):**
    - Use convolutional layers to perform pixel-wise classification.
  - **U-Net:**

- A popular architecture for biomedical image segmentation.
  - **Mask R-CNN:**
    - Extends Faster R-CNN to perform instance segmentation.

9.5 Applications of Computer Vision: Image Recognition, Medical Imaging, and More

Computer vision has a wide range of applications in various domains, including:

- **Image Recognition:**
  - Identifying and classifying objects in images.
  - Applications: Image search, object recognition, and facial recognition.[23]

- **Medical Imaging:**
  - Analyzing medical images (e.g., X-rays, CT scans, MRIs) for diagnosis and treatment planning.[24]
  - Applications: Cancer detection, disease diagnosis, and surgical planning.[25]
- **Autonomous Vehicles:**
  - Detecting and tracking objects in the environment for navigation and safety.
  - Applications: Lane detection, object detection, and traffic sign recognition.[26]
- **Surveillance:**
  - Monitoring and analyzing video streams for security and safety.
  - Applications: Object tracking, anomaly detection, and facial recognition.
- **Industrial Automation:**

- Inspecting products for defects and controlling robots for manufacturing.[27]
- Applications: Quality control, robotic vision, and process automation.[28]
- **Augmented Reality (AR) and Virtual Reality (VR):**
  - Overlaying digital information onto the real world and creating immersive virtual environments.
  - Applications: Gaming, education, and training.
- **Retail:**
  - Analyzing customer behavior and optimizing store layouts.[29]
  - Applications: Product recognition, shelf monitoring, and customer tracking.[30]
- **Agriculture:**
  - Monitoring crop health and detecting diseases.[31]

- Applications: Precision agriculture, crop monitoring, and weed detection.[32]
- **Robotics:**
  - Enabling robots to perceive and interact with their environment.[33]
  - Applications: navigation, object manipulation, and human-robot interaction.
- **Document Analysis:**
  - Optical Character Recognition(OCR), and document classification.[34]

By understanding CNNs, object detection, image segmentation, and the diverse applications of computer vision, you can build intelligent systems that perceive and interpret the visual world.

CHAPTER 10

Time Series Analysis and Forecasting

This field focuses on analyzing and predicting data points collected over time.[1] Key aspects include understanding time series characteristics (trend, seasonality, noise), decomposing data, and applying forecasting methods.[2] Statistical methods like ARIMA and exponential smoothing, along with machine learning approaches (regression, neural networks), are used to predict future values.[3] Proper evaluation and tuning are crucial for accurate forecasts, ensuring reliable insights and informed decision-making.[4]

10.1 Time Series Data: Concepts and Characteristics

Time series data is a sequence of data points collected or recorded at successive points in time.[1] It's a critical data type in various fields, from finance and economics to meteorology and healthcare.[2]

Key Concepts:

- **Time Index:** The ordered sequence of time points at which data is collected.
- **Regular Intervals:** Time series data is typically collected at regular intervals (e.g., hourly, daily, monthly, yearly).[3]
- **Ordering Matters:** The order of data points is crucial in time series analysis, as it reflects the temporal dependencies and patterns.[4]
- **Univariate vs. Multivariate:**

- Univariate: A single variable is measured over time (e.g., stock price).[5]
- Multivariate: Multiple variables are measured over time (e.g., temperature and humidity).[6]

Characteristics of Time Series Data:

- **Trend:** A long-term pattern or direction in the data. It can be upward, downward, or horizontal.
- **Seasonality:** A recurring pattern or fluctuation that occurs at regular intervals (e.g., daily, weekly, monthly, yearly).[7]
- **Cyclicity:** A pattern that repeats over irregular intervals, often longer than seasonal patterns.[8]
- **Irregularity (Noise):** Random fluctuations or disturbances in the

data that are not explained by trend, seasonality, or cyclicity.[9]

- **Stationarity:** A property of a time series where its statistical properties (mean, variance, autocorrelation) remain constant over time.[10]
  - Strict stationarity is very difficult to achieve. Usually we test for weak stationarity.
  - Stationarity is often a requirement for many time series forecasting models.[11]

-

- **Autocorrelation:** The correlation between a time series and its lagged values.[12]
- **Seasonality and Trend Interactions:** Seasonality can be additive or multiplicative with trend.

Why Time Series Analysis?

- **Forecasting:** Predicting future values based on historical data.[13]

- **Pattern Recognition:** Identifying trends, seasonality, and other patterns in the data.[14]
- **Anomaly Detection:** Detecting unusual or unexpected events in the data.[15]
- **Control and Optimization:** Optimizing processes and systems based on time series data.[16]

10.2 Time Series Decomposition: Trend, Seasonality, and Residuals

Time series decomposition is a technique that separates a time series into its constituent components: trend, seasonality, and residuals.[17]

Purpose of Decomposition:

- **Understanding Data:** Gaining insights into the underlying patterns and dynamics of the time series.[18]
- **Feature Extraction:** Extracting features that can be used for forecasting or other analysis.[19]
- **Model Selection:** Choosing appropriate forecasting models based on the characteristics of the components.
- **Removing noise:** Isolating the noise, or remainder of a time series.

Types of Decomposition:

- **Additive Decomposition:** Assumes that the components are added together:[20]
  - $y(t) = Trend(t) + Seasonality(t) + Residual(t)$
  - Suitable for time series with constant seasonal variations.
-

- **Multiplicative Decomposition:**
  Assumes that the components are
  multiplied together:[21]
  - $y(t) = Trend(t) * Seasonality(t) * Residual(t)$
  - Suitable for time series with
    seasonal variations that increase
    or decrease with the trend.
-

Methods for Decomposition:

- **Moving Average:**
  - Calculates the average of a
    specified number of consecutive
    data points.
  - Smooths out short-term
    fluctuations and reveals the
    trend.
  - pandas.Series.rolling(): Used to
    calculate moving averages.
- **Seasonal Decomposition of Time
  Series (STL):**

- A robust and versatile method for decomposing time series.[22]
- Uses locally weighted regression (LOESS) to estimate the trend and seasonal components.[23]
- Handles both additive and multiplicative seasonality.
- statsmodels.tsa.seasonal.seasonal_decompose(): Used to perform STL decomposition.

- **Classical Decomposition:**
  - A more simple method of decomposition.
  - Calculates the trend using moving averages, and then removes the trend to calculate seasonality.
  - Less robust than STL.

Steps in Decomposition:

1. **Choose Decomposition Type:** Determine whether additive or

multiplicative decomposition is appropriate.

2. **Estimate Trend:** Calculate the trend component using moving averages or other methods.
3. **Estimate Seasonality:** Calculate the seasonal component by removing the trend from the original time series.
4. **Calculate Residuals:** Calculate the residuals by subtracting the trend and seasonal components from the original time series.
5. **Visualize Components:** Plot the original time series and its decomposed components to gain insights.

Interpreting Components:

- **Trend:** Indicates the long-term direction of the time series.
- **Seasonality:** Reveals recurring patterns and their magnitude.[24]

- **Residuals:** Represents the random fluctuations and noise in the data.[25]

Applications:

- **Sales Forecasting:** Decomposing sales data to identify trends and seasonal patterns.[26]
- **Inventory Management:** Optimizing inventory levels based on seasonal demand.[27]
- **Economic Analysis:** Analyzing economic indicators to identify trends and cycles.[28]
- **Weather Forecasting:** Decomposing weather data to identify seasonal patterns and trends.[29]

By understanding the concepts and characteristics of time series data and mastering decomposition techniques, you can effectively analyze and forecast time series data in various domains.

10.3 Statistical Forecasting Methods: ARIMA and Exponential Smoothing

Statistical forecasting methods are traditional approaches that rely on statistical models to predict future values based on historical time series data.[1]

1. ARIMA (Autoregressive Integrated Moving Average):[2]

- **Purpose:** A powerful and widely used method for forecasting stationary or non-stationary time series data.[3]
- **Components:**
    1. **Autoregressive (AR):** Models the relationship between a time series and its lagged values.[4]
    2. **Integrated (I):** Makes a non-stationary time series stationary by differencing.[5]

3. **Moving Average (MA):** Models the relationship between a time series and its past forecast errors.

- **Parameters:**
  1. **p (AR order):** The number of lagged values used in the AR component.[6]
  2. **d (Differencing order):** The number of times the data is differenced to achieve stationarity.[7]
  3. **q (MA order):** The number of lagged forecast errors used in the MA component.[8]

- **Steps:**
  1. **Stationarity Testing:** Check if the time series is stationary using tests like the Augmented Dickey-Fuller (ADF) test.[9]
  2. **Differencing:** If the series is non-stationary, difference it until it becomes stationary.

3. **Parameter Selection:** Determine the optimal values of p, d, and q using autocorrelation function (ACF) and partial autocorrelation function (PACF) plots, or using automated techniques.[10]
4. **Model Fitting:** Fit the ARIMA model to the data.
5. **Forecasting:** Generate forecasts using the fitted model.

- **Implementation:** statsmodels.tsa.arima.model.ARIMA

Exponential Smoothing:

- **Purpose:** A family of forecasting methods that assign exponentially decreasing weights to past observations.[11]
- **Types:**
  1. **Simple Exponential Smoothing:** Suitable for time

series with no trend or seasonality.

2. **Holt's Linear Trend Method:** Suitable for time series with trend but no seasonality.

3. **Holt-Winters' Seasonal Method:** Suitable for time series with both trend and seasonality.

- **Parameters:**
  1. **Alpha (α):** Smoothing parameter for the level.
  2. **Beta (β):** Smoothing parameter for the trend.
  3. **Gamma (γ):** Smoothing parameter for the seasonality.

- **Steps:**
  1. **Select Method:** Choose the appropriate exponential smoothing method based on the characteristics of the data.

2. **Parameter Selection:** Determine the optimal values of the smoothing parameters.
3. **Model Fitting:** Fit the exponential smoothing model to the data.
4. **Forecasting:** Generate forecasts using the fitted model.
- **Implementation:** statsmodels.tsa.holtwinters.Exponenti alSmoothing

10.4 Machine Learning for Time Series Forecasting: Regression and Neural Networks

Machine learning algorithms can also be used for time series forecasting, offering flexibility and the ability to capture complex patterns.[12]

Regression-Based Methods:

- **Purpose:** Transform time series data into a supervised learning problem by creating lagged features.
- **Steps:**
  - **Feature Engineering:** Create lagged features by shifting the time series data.
  - **Data Splitting:** Split the data into training and test sets.
  - **Model Selection:** Choose a regression algorithm (e.g., linear regression, random forest, gradient boosting).
  - **Model Training:** Train the regression model on the training data.
  - **Forecasting:** Generate forecasts using the trained model.
- **Advantages:**
  - Can capture non-linear relationships.
  - Flexible and adaptable to different time series patterns.[13]

- **Disadvantages:**
  - Requires careful feature engineering.
  - Can be sensitive to outliers.

Neural Networks:

- **Purpose:** Use neural network architectures like Recurrent Neural Networks (RNNs) and Long Short-Term Memory (LSTM) networks to model temporal dependencies.[14]
- **Steps:**
  - **Data Preprocessing:** Scale and normalize the time series data.
  - **Data Transformation:** Transform the data into a sequence of input-output pairs.
  - **Model Architecture:** Define the RNN or LSTM architecture.

- ○ **Model Training:** Train the neural network on the training data.
- ○ **Forecasting:** Generate forecasts using the trained model.
- **Advantages:**
  - ○ Can capture complex, non-linear patterns and long-term dependencies.
  - ○ Can handle multivariate time series data.
- **Disadvantages:**
  - ○ Requires significant computational resources.
  - ○ Can be challenging to tune hyperparameters.
  - ○ Can overfit if not properly regularized.

10.5 Evaluating and Tuning Time Series Models

Evaluating and tuning time series models is crucial to ensure accurate and reliable forecasts.

Evaluation Metrics:

- **Mean Absolute Error (MAE):** The average absolute difference between predicted and actual values.[15]
- **Mean Squared Error (MSE):** The average squared difference between predicted and actual values.[16]
- **Root Mean Squared Error (RMSE):** The square root of MSE.[17][18]
- **Mean Absolute Percentage Error (MAPE):** The average percentage difference between predicted and actual values.[19]
- **Symmetric Mean Absolute Percentage Error (sMAPE):** A

modified version of MAPE that is symmetric around zero.

Evaluation Techniques:

- **Train-Test Split:** Split the data into training and test sets, ensuring that the test set is chronologically after the training set.
- **Cross-Validation:** Use time series cross-validation techniques, such as rolling forecast origin cross-validation, to evaluate model performance.[20]
- **Walk-Forward Validation:** Train the model on the initial data, make a forecast, add the actual value to the training data, and repeat the process.[21]

Hyperparameter Tuning:

- **Grid Search:** Exhaustively search over a predefined set of hyperparameter values.

- **Random Search:** Randomly sample hyperparameter values from a predefined distribution.[22]
- **Bayesian Optimization:** Use Bayesian optimization to efficiently search for optimal hyperparameter values.[23]
- **Automated ARIMA (auto-ARIMA):** Use automated techniques to select the optimal ARIMA parameters.
- **Tools:** pmdarima.auto_arima for automated ARIMA, scikit-learn for grid and random search, and optuna for Bayesian optimization.

Key Considerations:

- **Stationarity:** Ensure that the time series is stationary before applying ARIMA or other statistical methods.
- **Seasonality:** Account for seasonality in the data by using appropriate methods or parameters.

- **Feature Engineering:** Create relevant features, such as lagged values or seasonal indicators, to improve model performance.
- **Model Selection:** Choose the appropriate forecasting method based on the characteristics of the data and the forecasting horizon.
- **Validation:** Validate the model's performance on unseen data to ensure generalization.
- **Forecast Horizon:** The number of time steps into the future to forecast.[24]
- **Rolling Forecasts:** Using a rolling forecast origin, where the model is retrained with new data as it becomes available.[25]

By mastering statistical and machine learning methods, and understanding the importance of proper evaluation and tuning, you can build accurate and reliable time series forecasting models.

CHAPTER 11

Recommender Systems

Recommender systems personalize user experiences by suggesting relevant items. They utilize techniques like collaborative filtering (user/item similarity) and content-based filtering (item features). These systems are crucial for enhancing engagement, driving discovery, and mitigating information overload in various online platforms.

11.1 Introduction to Recommender Systems: Collaborative Filtering and Content-Based Filtering

Recommender systems have become indispensable in the digital age, shaping user experiences across various platforms.[1] Their primary goal is to predict and suggest items that users are likely to find interesting or useful, thereby enhancing engagement, discovery, and overall satisfaction.[2]

The Necessity of Recommender Systems:

In the era of information overload, users face the daunting task of navigating vast catalogs of products, services, and content.[3] Recommender systems act as intelligent filters, streamlining the decision-making process by:

- **Personalizing   Experiences:** Tailoring suggestions to individual preferences and behaviors.[4]
- **Boosting   Engagement:** Encouraging users to explore and interact with relevant content.[5]
- **Driving Discovery:** Introducing users to items they might not have otherwise encountered.[6]
- **Increasing   Conversions:** Promoting products and services that align with user interests, leading to higher conversion rates.[7]
- **Mitigating Choice Paralysis:** Reducing the cognitive load associated with sifting through numerous options.

Fundamental   Approaches   to Recommendation:

1. **Collaborative Filtering (CF):**

- Core **Principle:** CF leverages the collective wisdom of users to make recommendations.[8] It operates on the assumption that users with similar preferences will likely have similar tastes.
- **Data Reliance:** CF primarily relies on user-item interaction data, such as ratings, purchase history, viewing patterns, or click-through rates.[9]
- **Abstraction of Item Features:** Notably, CF does not require explicit information about the features or attributes of the items themselves.[10] It focuses on the patterns of user behavior.
- **Types:**
  - User-based CF: Recommends items based on the preferences of similar users.[11]

- Item-based CF: Recommends items based on the similarity between items.[12]
- **Strengths:**
  - Ability to discover novel and unexpected items.
  - Effective in domains where item features are difficult to define or extract.
- **Weaknesses:**
  - Susceptibility to sparsity issues (when user-item interaction data is sparse).[13]
  - Scalability challenges with large user bases.
  - Vulnerability to the "cold-start" problem (difficulty recommending to new users or items).[14]

2. **Content-Based Filtering (CBF):**

- **Core Principle:** CBF recommends items that are similar to those a user has liked in the past, based on the inherent features of the items.[15]
- **Feature Reliance:** CBF relies on explicit information about the features or attributes of the items, such as genre, keywords, descriptions, or tags.[16]
- **User Profiling:** CBF builds user profiles based on their past interactions and preferences, representing their interests in terms of item features.[17]
- **Strengths:**
  - Ability to provide transparent and explainable recommendations.
  - Effective in domains where item features are readily available.

- Capability to address the cold-start problem for new users (if item features are available).[18]
- **Weaknesses:**
  - Limited ability to discover novel or serendipitous items.
  - Requirement for detailed item feature information.
  - Susceptibility to over-specialization (recommending only items similar to those already liked).

11.2 User-Based and Item-Based Collaborative Filtering

Collaborative filtering, a cornerstone of recommender systems, offers two primary approaches: user-based and item-based.[19]

1. User-Based Collaborative Filtering:

- **Conceptual Foundation:**
  - The fundamental idea is to identify users who exhibit similar preferences to the target user and then recommend items that these similar users have liked.[20]
  - "Birds of a feather flock together" analogy.
- **Detailed Process:**
  - **User Similarity Computation:**
    - Calculate the similarity between users based on their historical

interactions, typically ratings.

- Common similarity measures include:
    - Cosine similarity: Measures the angle between user rating vectors.[21]
    - Pearson correlation: Measures the linear correlation between user ratings.[22]
    - Jaccard similarity: Measures the overlap between sets of items rated by users.
- **Neighborhood Formation:**
    - Select the k most similar users (the k-nearest neighbors) to the target user.
- **Rating Prediction:**

- Predict the target user's rating for an item by aggregating the ratings of their neighbors, often using a weighted average.[23]
  - **Recommendation Generation:**
    - Recommend items with the highest predicted ratings.
- **Advantages:**
  - Intuitive and easily understandable.
  - Effective in discovering novel items that the user might not have considered.
- **Disadvantages:**
  - Scalability limitations, as computing user similarities for large user bases can be computationally expensive.[24]
  - Sensitivity to data sparsity, where many users have rated only a small subset of items.[25]

○ Cold start issues for new users.

2. Item-Based Collaborative Filtering:

- **Conceptual Foundation:**
  ○ The focus shifts from user similarity to item similarity.[26]
  ○ The system recommends items that are similar to those the user has positively interacted with.
  ○ "People who liked this item also liked..."
- **Detailed Process:**
  ○ **Item Similarity Computation:**
    ■ Calculate the similarity between items based on user ratings.
    ■ Common similarity measures include cosine similarity and adjusted cosine similarity (which

accounts for user rating biases).[27]

- **Neighborhood Formation:**
  - Identify the k most similar items to those the user has liked.
- **Rating Prediction:**
  - Predict the user's rating for an item by aggregating their ratings of similar items.[28]
- **Recommendation Generation:**
  - Recommend items with the highest predicted ratings.

- **Advantages:**
  - Improved scalability compared to user-based CF, as item similarities are generally more stable.[29]
  - Better handling of sparse data.
  - More stable recommendations.
- **Disadvantages:**

- Reduced ability to discover novel items, as recommendations tend to be closely related to the user's past preferences.
- Cold start issues for new items.

Key Differences and Considerations:

- **Scalability:** Item-based CF is generally more scalable due to the relatively static nature of item similarities.
- **Discovery:** User-based CF can be more effective in discovering novel items.
- **Sparsity:** Item-based CF tends to be more robust to data sparsity.[30]
- **Computational Complexity:** Item-based CF often requires less computational resources for recommendation generation.[31]

- **Data Dynamics:** User preferences can change more rapidly than item features, making item-based CF more stable.

By understanding the nuances of collaborative and content-based filtering, along with the specifics of user-based and item-based CF, you can make informed decisions about the most appropriate recommendation strategy for a given application.

11.3 Matrix Factorization: Singular Value Decomposition (SVD) and Alternating Least Squares (ALS)

Matrix factorization is a powerful technique used in recommender systems to uncover latent factors that explain user-item interactions.[1] It addresses the sparsity and scalability challenges of traditional collaborative filtering.[2]

Key Concepts:

- **User-Item Interaction Matrix:** Represents user ratings or interactions with items.[3] It's often sparse, with many missing values.[4]
- **Latent Factors:** Hidden features or attributes that characterize users and items.
- **Factorization:** Decomposing the user-item matrix into two

lower-dimensional matrices: user latent factor matrix and item latent factor matrix.[5]

- **Prediction:** Approximating the missing values in the user-item matrix by multiplying the user and item latent factor matrices.[6]

1. Singular Value Decomposition (SVD):

- **Principle:** Decomposes a matrix into three matrices: U (left singular vectors), Σ (singular values), and V^T (right singular vectors).
- **Application in Recommender Systems:**
  - The user-item matrix is approximated by the product of U, Σ, and V^T.
  - The latent factors are represented by the columns of U and V.

- The singular values in Σ represent the importance of each latent factor.
- **Challenges:**
  - SVD requires a complete matrix, which is not the case in recommender systems (due to sparsity).
  - Imputation techniques are needed to fill in missing values, which can introduce bias.
  - Computational cost can be high for large matrices.[7]
- **Truncated SVD:** A variant of SVD that retains only the top k singular values and vectors, reducing dimensionality and computational cost.[8]
- **Implementation:** scikit-learn.decomposition.Truncated SVD

2. Alternating Least Squares (ALS):

- **Principle:** An iterative optimization algorithm that minimizes the squared error between the predicted and actual ratings.
- **Process:**
  - **Initialization:** Initialize the user and item latent factor matrices randomly.
  - **User Factor Update:** Fix the item factors and update the user factors by minimizing the error.
  - **Item Factor Update:** Fix the user factors and update the item factors by minimizing the error.
  - **Iteration:** Repeat steps 2 and 3 until convergence.
- **Advantages:**
  - Can handle sparse matrices efficiently.
  - Scalable to large datasets.
  - Can be implemented in parallel.
- **Implementation:** Libraries like implicit and Spark MLlib provide ALS implementations.

- **Regularization:** ALS typically includes regularization terms to prevent overfitting.
- **Implicit Feedback:** ALS can be adapted to handle implicit feedback (e.g., clicks, purchases) by using weighted least squares or other techniques.

11.4 Building Hybrid Recommender Systems

Hybrid recommender systems combine multiple recommendation techniques to leverage their strengths and mitigate their weaknesses.[9]

Why Hybrid Systems?

- **Improve Accuracy:** Combine the strengths of different techniques to achieve higher accuracy.

- **Address Cold Start:** Use content-based or demographic information to address the cold-start problem.
- **Enhance Diversity:** Introduce diversity into recommendations by combining different approaches.
- **Improve Coverage:** Increase the coverage of recommendations by using multiple techniques.

Hybrid Approaches:

- **Weighted Hybrid:** Combine the predictions of multiple recommenders by assigning weights to each.
- **Switching Hybrid:** Select the best recommender for a given situation or user.
- **Mixed Hybrid:** Combine the recommendations of multiple recommenders into a single list.

- **Feature Combination Hybrid:** Combine the features of different techniques into a single model.
- **Cascade Hybrid:** Use one recommender to refine the recommendations of another.

Examples of Hybrid Systems:

- **Content-Boosted Collaborative Filtering:** Use content-based information to improve collaborative filtering.
- **Demographic-Based Collaborative Filtering:** Use demographic information to improve collaborative filtering.
- **Knowledge-Based Collaborative Filtering:** Use knowledge graphs or domain knowledge to improve collaborative filtering.
- **Deep Learning Hybrid:** Combine deep learning models with traditional recommendation techniques.

11.5 Evaluating Recommender Systems and Addressing Cold Start Problems

Evaluating recommender systems and addressing the cold-start problem are crucial for building effective and user-friendly systems.

Evaluation Metrics:

- **Accuracy Metrics:**
  - **Root Mean Squared Error (RMSE):** Measures the difference between predicted and actual ratings.[10]
  - **Mean Absolute Error (MAE):** Measures the average absolute difference between predicted and actual ratings.[11]
- **Ranking Metrics:**

- ○ **Precision@k:** Measures the proportion of relevant items in the top k recommendations.[12]
- ○ **Recall@k:** Measures the proportion of relevant items that are in the top k recommendations.[13]
- ○ **F1-score@k:** The harmonic mean of precision@k and recall@k.
- ○ **Mean Average Precision (MAP):** Measures the average precision across all users.
- ○ **Normalized Discounted Cumulative Gain (NDCG):** Measures the ranking quality of recommendations.[14]
- **Diversity Metrics:**
  - ○ **Intralist Similarity:** Measures the similarity between items in the recommendation list.[15]
  - ○ **Coverage:** Measures the proportion of items that are recommended.

- **Novelty Metrics:**
  - **Serendipity:** Measures the unexpectedness and relevance of recommendations.[16]
- **User Satisfaction Metrics:**
  - **Click-Through Rate (CTR):** Measures the proportion of users who click on recommendations.[17]
  - **Conversion Rate:** Measures the proportion of users who complete a desired action after clicking on recommendations.
  - **User Surveys:** Collect user feedback on the quality of recommendations.

Evaluation Techniques:

- **Offline Evaluation:** Evaluate the model on historical data using metrics like RMSE, precision, and recall.[18]

- **Online Evaluation (A/B Testing):** Deploy the model to a subset of users and compare its performance to a baseline model.
- **Cross-Validation:** Use techniques like k-fold cross-validation to evaluate model performance on different subsets of the data.[1920]

Addressing Cold Start Problems:

- **Cold Start for New Users:**
  - **Content-Based Filtering:** Use user profile information or demographic data to make initial recommendations.
  - **Hybrid Approaches:** Combine collaborative filtering with content-based or demographic information.[21]
  - **Ask for Preferences:** Ask new users to rate a few items or provide their preferences.
- **Cold Start for New Items:**

- Content-Based Filtering: Use item features to make initial recommendations.
- Hybrid Approaches: Combine collaborative filtering with content-based information.[22]
- Popularity-Based Recommendations: Recommend popular items to new users.

- **Contextual Information:**
  - Incorporate contextual information, such as time, location, and device, to improve recommendations.
- **Active Learning:**
  - Select the most informative items to ask users to rate.
- **Knowledge Graphs:**
  - Use knowledge graphs to infer relationships between users and items.

By mastering matrix factorization, building hybrid systems, and understanding the evaluation and cold-start challenges, you can develop robust and effective recommender systems that enhance user experiences and drive business value.

CHAPTER 12

Model Evaluation and Hyperparameter Tuning

These processes are vital for building effective machine learning models. Model evaluation uses metrics like accuracy, precision, recall, and ROC curves to assess performance. Cross-validation ensures robust generalization. Hyperparameter tuning, using methods like grid, random, or Bayesian search, optimizes model settings. The bias-variance tradeoff guides model selection, balancing underfitting and overfitting. Techniques like regularization and early stopping prevent these issues, ensuring models perform well on unseen data.

12.1 Performance Metrics: Accuracy, Precision, Recall, F1-Score, and ROC Curves

Evaluating the performance of a machine learning model is essential to ensure its effectiveness and generalization ability.[1] Different metrics are used depending on the type of problem and the specific goals of the analysis.

1. Accuracy:

- **Definition:** The proportion of correctly classified instances out of the total number of instances.[2]
- **Formula:** Accuracy = (True Positives + True Negatives) / (Total Instances)
- **Use Case:** Suitable for balanced datasets where all classes are equally important.
- **Limitations:** Can be misleading for imbalanced datasets, where one class dominates.[3]

2. Precision:

- **Definition:** The proportion of correctly predicted positive instances out of all instances predicted as positive.[4]
- **Formula:** Precision = True Positives / (True Positives + False Positives)[56]
- **Use Case:** Important when minimizing false positives is crucial (e.g., spam detection, medical diagnosis).[7]

3. Recall (Sensitivity):

- **Definition:** The proportion of correctly predicted positive instances out of all actual positive instances.
- **Formula:** Recall = True Positives / (True Positives + False Negatives)[8]
- **Use Case:** Important when minimizing false negatives is crucial (e.g., fraud detection, disease detection).

4. F1-Score:

- **Definition:** The harmonic mean of precision and recall, providing a balanced measure of both.[9]
- **Formula:** F1-Score = 2 * (Precision * Recall) / (Precision + Recall)
- **Use Case:** Suitable when both precision and recall are important, especially for imbalanced datasets.

5. ROC Curves (Receiver Operating Characteristic Curves):

- **Definition:** A graphical representation of the trade-off between true positive rate (recall) and false positive rate at various threshold settings.[1011]
- **Area Under the Curve (AUC):** A single value that summarizes the overall performance of the model.
- **Use Case:** Suitable for binary classification problems, especially

when evaluating the performance of probabilistic models.

- **Interpretation:** An AUC of 1 indicates perfect performance, while an AUC of 0.5 indicates random guessing.[12]

12.2 Cross-Validation: Evaluating Model Generalization

Cross-validation is a robust technique for evaluating the generalization performance of a model by partitioning the data into multiple folds and training and evaluating the model on different combinations of folds.[13]

Types of Cross-Validation:

- **k-Fold Cross-Validation:**
  - The data is partitioned into k equal-sized folds.

- The model is trained on k-1 folds and evaluated on the remaining fold.[14]
- This process is repeated k times, with each fold serving as the validation set[15] once.[16]
- The average performance across all folds is used as[17] the overall evaluation metric.

- **Stratified k-Fold Cross-Validation:**
  - Similar to k-fold cross-validation, but ensures that the class distribution is preserved in each fold.
  - Suitable for imbalanced datasets.

- **Leave-One-Out Cross-Validation (LOOCV):**
  - Each instance is used as the validation set once, and the model is trained on the remaining instances.

- ○ Can be computationally expensive for large datasets.
- **Time Series Cross-Validation:**
  - ○ Used for time series data, where the order of data points is crucial.
  - ○ Ensures that the validation set is chronologically after the training set.

Benefits of Cross-Validation:

- Provides a more reliable estimate of model generalization performance.
- Reduces the risk of overfitting by evaluating the model on multiple subsets of the data.[18]
- Allows for better model selection and hyperparameter tuning.

12.3 Hyperparameter Tuning: Grid Search, Random Search, and Bayesian Optimization

Hyperparameters are parameters that are set before training a model, affecting its performance.[19] Hyperparameter tuning involves finding the optimal combination of hyperparameters that maximizes the model's performance.[20]

1. Grid Search:

- **Process:** Exhaustively searches over a predefined set of hyperparameter values.[21]
- **Advantages:** Guarantees finding the optimal combination within the specified search space.
- **Disadvantages:** Can be computationally expensive for large search spaces.

2. Random Search:

- **Process:** Randomly samples hyperparameter values from a predefined distribution.[22]
- **Advantages:** More efficient than grid search for high-dimensional hyperparameter spaces.[23]
- **Disadvantages:** May not find the optimal combination if the search space is not well-defined.

3. Bayesian Optimization:

- **Process:** Uses Bayesian inference to build a probabilistic model of the objective function and uses it to guide the search for optimal hyperparameters.[24]
- **Advantages:** More efficient than grid and random search, especially for expensive objective functions.[25]

- **Disadvantages:** Requires careful selection of the prior distribution and the acquisition function.

Tools for Hyperparameter Tuning:

- Scikit-learn's GridSearchCV and RandomizedSearchCV.
- Optuna.[26]
- Hyperopt.

12.4 Bias-Variance Tradeoff and Model Selection

The bias-variance tradeoff is a fundamental concept in machine learning that describes the relationship between bias, variance, and[27] model complexity.[28]

- **Bias:** The error introduced by approximating a real-world problem, which may be complex, by a simplified model. High bias can lead to underfitting.[2930]

- **Variance:** The variability of a model's predictions for different training datasets. High variance indicates that the model is sensitive to small fluctuations in the training data, leading to overfitting.[31]
- **Model Selection:** Choosing the model with the appropriate level of complexity to minimize both bias and variance.

12.5 Preventing Overfitting and Underfitting

Overfitting and underfitting are common problems that can affect the performance of machine learning models.[32]

Overfitting:

- **Definition:** A model that performs well on the training data but poorly on unseen data.[33]
- **Causes:** High model complexity, small training datasets, noisy data.
- **Techniques to Prevent Overfitting:**
  - **Regularization:** Adding a penalty term to the loss function to discourage complex models.[34]
  - **Dropout:** Randomly dropping out neurons during training to prevent co-adaptation.[35]
  - **Early Stopping:** Stopping training when the model's performance on a validation set stops improving.[36]
  - **Data Augmentation:** Increasing the size of the training dataset by generating synthetic data.[37]
  - **Cross-Validation:** Evaluating the model on multiple subsets of the data.[38]

Underfitting:

- **Definition:** A model that performs poorly on both the training data and unseen data.
- **Causes:** Low model complexity, insufficient training data, irrelevant features.
- **Techniques to Prevent Underfitting:**
  - **Increase Model Complexity:** Using a more complex model architecture.
  - **Feature Engineering:** Creating relevant features from the existing data.
  - **Increase Training Data:** Gathering more training data.
  - **Reduce Regularization:** Reducing the strength of regularization.

By understanding the performance metrics, cross-validation, hyperparameter tuning, bias-variance tradeoff, and techniques to prevent overfitting and underfitting, you can build robust and effective machine learning models that generalize well to unseen data.

CHAPTER 13

Deploying Machine Learning Models

Deploying ML models involves packaging (Pickle/Joblib), web app development (Flask/FastAPI), cloud deployment (AWS/GCP/Azure), containerization (Docker), and ongoing monitoring.[1] Packaging serializes models for storage.[2] Web apps expose models as APIs.[3] Cloud platforms offer scalable infrastructure.[4] Docker ensures consistent deployments.[5] Monitoring tracks performance and data drift, while maintenance includes retraining and updates.[6] These steps are crucial for making ML models accessible and reliable in production.[7]

Deploying a machine learning model is the transition from a research or development phase to a production environment where the model can provide value to users or systems.[1] This process involves several critical steps, each requiring careful consideration and execution.[2]

13.1 Packaging Machine Learning Models with Pickle and Joblib

Before a model can be deployed, it must be serialized, or packaged, to preserve its learned state.[3] This allows the model to be loaded and used in a different environment without retraining.

1. Pickle: Python's Native Serialization

- **Functionality:**
    - pickle is a standard Python module that enables the serialization and deserialization of Python object structures.

- It converts a Python object into a byte stream, which can be stored in a file or transmitted over a network.[4]
- **Usage:**
  - For simple models and smaller deployments, pickle provides a straightforward solution.
  - It's particularly useful when dealing with Python-specific objects and data structures.
- **Code Example:**
- Python

```python
import pickle

# Saving the model
with open('my_model.pkl', 'wb') as file:
    pickle.dump(my_trained_model, file)

# Loading the model
with open('my_model.pkl', 'rb') as file:
    loaded_model = pickle.load(file)
```

-
-
- **Caveats:**
  - Security risks: Loading pickled data from untrusted sources can execute arbitrary code.[5]
  - Version compatibility: Pickled objects may not be compatible across different Python versions.
  - Performance: For large models, pickle can be slow and memory-intensive.

2. Joblib: Optimized Serialization for NumPy and Machine Learning[6]

- **Functionality:**
  - joblib is a library designed to provide efficient serialization for large NumPy arrays and machine learning models.
  - It optimizes serialization and deserialization for numerical

data, making it faster and more memory-efficient than pickle.

- **Usage:**
  - Ideal for large models, especially those involving NumPy arrays or scikit-learn estimators.[7]
  - Provides caching mechanisms to speed up repeated computations.
- **Code Example:**
- Python

```python
import joblib

# Saving the model
joblib.dump(my_trained_model, 'my_model.joblib')

# Loading the model
loaded_model = joblib.load('my_model.joblib')
```

-
-
- **Advantages:**
  - ○ Significant performance improvements for large numerical datasets.
  - ○ Built-in support for compressing serialized files.
  - ○ Parallel processing capabilities.

13.2 Building Web Applications with Flask or FastAPI for Model Deployment

To make machine learning models accessible to users or other applications, they are often deployed as web APIs.[8] Flask and FastAPI are popular Python frameworks for this purpose.

1. Flask: A Microframework for Web Development

- **Characteristics:**
  - Flask is a lightweight and flexible web framework that allows developers to build web applications with minimal overhead.[9]
  - It provides essential tools for routing requests, handling HTTP methods, and rendering responses.
- **Usage:**
  - Suitable for building simple to medium-sized web applications and APIs.
  - Provides a good balance between simplicity and flexibility.
- **Code Example:**
- Python

```
from flask import Flask, request, jsonify
import joblib

app = Flask(__name__)
```

```python
model = joblib.load('my_model.joblib')

@app.route('/predict', methods=['POST'])
def predict():
    data = request.get_json()
    features = data['features']
    prediction = model.predict([features]).tolist()
    return jsonify({'prediction': prediction})

if __name__ == '__main__':
    app.run(debug=True)
```

-
-
- **Advantages:**
  - Easy to learn and use.
  - Large community and extensive documentation.
  - Extensible with a wide range of extensions.

2. FastAPI: A Modern, High-Performance Web Framework

- **Characteristics:**
  - ○ FastAPI is a modern, high-performance web framework for building APIs with Python.[10]
  - ○ It leverages type hints and asynchronous programming to achieve high performance and developer productivity.
  - ○ Automatic interactive API documentation.
- **Usage:**
  - ○ Ideal for building high-performance APIs and microservices.
  - ○ Provides automatic data validation and serialization.
- **Code Example:**
- Python

```python
from fastapi import FastAPI
import joblib

app = FastAPI()
model = joblib.load('my_model.joblib')

@app.post('/predict')
async def predict(features: list):
                            prediction       =
model.predict([features]).tolist()
   return {'prediction': prediction}
```

-
-
- **Advantages:**
  - Exceptional performance.
  - Automatic API documentation with Swagger UI.
  - Type hints and data validation for improved code quality.
  - Asynchronous capabilities.

13.3 Deploying Models on Cloud Platforms (AWS, Google Cloud, Azure)

Cloud platforms offer scalable and reliable infrastructure for deploying machine learning models, providing services for model serving, infrastructure management, and monitoring.[11]

1. AWS (Amazon Web Services):

- **Services:**
  - Amazon SageMaker: A fully managed machine learning service that simplifies the process of building, training, and deploying[12] models.[13]
  - AWS Lambda: A serverless computing service that allows you to run code without provisioning or managing servers.[14]

- ○ Amazon EC2: Provides virtual servers in the cloud for running applications.[15]
- **Advantages:**
  - ○ Comprehensive suite of machine learning and infrastructure services.
  - ○ Global infrastructure and high availability.
  - ○ Extensive documentation and community support.

2. Google Cloud Platform (GCP):

- **Services:**
  - ○ Vertex AI: A unified platform for building, training, and deploying machine learning models.[16]
  - ○ Cloud Functions: A serverless execution environment for building and connecting cloud services.[17]

- Compute Engine: Virtual machines that let you run workloads on Google's infrastructure.[18]
- **Advantages:**
  - Strong integration with Google's AI and data analytics ecosystem.
  - Competitive pricing and flexible compute options.
  - User-friendly interface and comprehensive documentation.

3. Azure (Microsoft Azure):

- **Services:**
  - Azure Machine Learning: A cloud-based environment for building, training, and deploying machine learning models.[19]
  - Azure Functions: A serverless compute service that enables you to run event-triggered code without having to explicitly

provision or manage infrastructure.[2021]

- ○ Azure Virtual Machines: On-demand, scalable computing resources that give you the flexibility of virtualization.[22]

- **Advantages:**
  - ○ Seamless integration with Microsoft's ecosystem.
  - ○ Enterprise-grade security and compliance features.
  - ○ Hybrid cloud capabilities.

13.4 Containerization with Docker for Scalable Deployments

Docker is a containerization platform that allows you to package applications and their dependencies into lightweight, portable containers.[2324] This ensures consistent deployment across different environments.

Key Concepts:

- **Docker Image:** A read-only template with instructions for creating a Docker container.[25]
- **Docker Container:** A running instance of a Docker image.[26]
- **Dockerfile:** A text file that contains instructions for building a Docker image.[27]

Benefits of Docker:

- **Portability:** Containers can run on any platform that supports Docker.[28]
- **Consistency:** Ensures that the application runs in the same environment across different systems.
- **Scalability:** Allows for easy scaling of applications by running multiple containers.[29]
- **Isolation:** Containers provide isolation between applications, preventing conflicts.[30]

- **Reproducibility:** Docker images can be used to reproduce the same environment for development, testing, and production.[31]

13.5 Monitoring and Maintaining Deployed Models

The deployment of a machine learning model marks a significant milestone, but it's not the endpoint. Real-world environments are dynamic, and models, like any other software system, require continuous oversight and upkeep. The success of a deployed model hinges on its ability to adapt to evolving data patterns, maintain performance standards, and seamlessly integrate with the broader system.[1]

The Indispensable Role of Monitoring and Maintenance:

- **Preserving Model Integrity:**

- Models are trained on specific datasets, and their performance is optimized for those conditions. However, real-world data is often subject to change, leading to *data drift*.[2]
- *Concept drift* occurs when the underlying relationship between input features and target variables shifts, rendering the model's learned patterns obsolete.
- Monitoring these drifts is crucial for preserving the model's predictive accuracy.[3]
- **Ensuring Operational Reliability:**
  - Models are deployed within complex systems, and their performance can be affected by infrastructure issues, software bugs, or security vulnerabilities.[4]
  - Continuous monitoring helps identify and mitigate these issues promptly.[5]

- **Adapting to Evolving Requirements:**
  - Business needs and user preferences can change, requiring model updates or modifications.
  - Monitoring provides insights into these changes, enabling timely adjustments to the model.[6]
- **Building Trust and Transparency:**
  - Monitoring provides evidence of the model's performance and reliability, fostering trust among stakeholders.[7]
  - Logging and auditing capabilities enhance transparency and accountability.

The Landscape of Monitoring:

1. **Performance Monitoring: Keeping Score:**
   - **Metric Tracking:**
     - Define key performance indicators (KPIs) relevant to the model's task.
     - For classification: accuracy, precision, recall, F1-score, ROC-AUC.
     - For regression: MSE, RMSE, MAE.
     - Automate the collection and tracking of these metrics.
   - **Alerting:**
     - Establish thresholds for acceptable performance levels.[8]
     - Configure alerts to notify stakeholders when metrics fall below these thresholds.[9]
   - **Visualization:**

- Create dashboards and visualizations to monitor performance trends over time.
- Identify patterns and anomalies that may indicate issues.

2. **Data Monitoring: The Pulse of Input Data:**
   - **Distribution Monitoring:**
     - Track the statistical properties of input features (mean, variance, distribution).[10]
     - Detect data drift using statistical tests (e.g., Kolmogorov-Smirnov test).[11]
   - **Anomaly Detection:**
     - Identify outliers or anomalies in the input data using techniques like isolation forests or clustering.[12]

- Investigate anomalies to determine their cause and impact.
  - **Feature Monitoring:**
    - Track feature usage and importance.
    - Identify changes in feature relevance.
3. **Latency and Resource Monitoring: The Operational Backbone:**
   - **Latency:**
     - Monitor the response time of the model's predictions.
     - Ensure that the model meets performance requirements.
   - **Throughput:**
     - Track the number of requests processed per unit of time.
     - Assess the model's capacity and scalability.
   - **Resource Usage:**

- Monitor CPU, memory, and network usage.
- Identify resource bottlenecks and optimize performance.

4. **Logging: The Trail of Evidence:**
   - **Prediction Logging:**
     - Log model predictions, input features, and timestamps.
     - Facilitate auditing, debugging, and analysis.
   - **Error Logging:**
     - Log errors and exceptions.
     - Identify and resolve issues quickly.
   - **Audit Logging:**
     - Log user actions and system events.
     - Enhance security and compliance.

The Practices of Maintenance:

1. **Model Retraining: Staying Current:**
   o **Periodic Retraining:**
     ■ Retrain the model at regular intervals to incorporate new data.[13]
   o **Triggered Retraining:**
     ■ Retrain the model when performance degrades or data drift is detected.[14]
   o **Incremental Retraining:**
     ■ Update the model with new data without retraining from scratch.
2. **Model Updating: Evolving with Change:**
   o **Feature Updates:**
     ■ Add, remove, or modify input features.
   o **Algorithm Updates:**

- Replace the model with a new algorithm or architecture.
  - **Hyperparameter Tuning:**
    - Fine-tune hyperparameters to optimize performance.[15]

3. **Version Control: The Safety Net:**
   - **Model Versioning:**
     - Track changes to the model's code, data, and configuration.
   - **Deployment Versioning:**
     - Track changes to the deployment environment.
   - **Rollback Capabilities:**
     - Implement mechanisms to revert to previous versions.

4. **Security Updates: Protecting the System:**
   - **Patching:**
     - Apply security patches to the operating system,

libraries, and frameworks.[16]

- ○ **Vulnerability Scanning:**
  - Regularly scan for security vulnerabilities.
- ○ **Access Control:**
  - Implement strong access control policies.

5. **Alerting and Incident Response: Reacting to Problems:**
   - ○ **Alerting System:**
     - Set up alerts for performance degradation, errors, or anomalies.
   - ○ **Incident Response Plan:**
     - Develop a plan to address and resolve issues promptly.

6. **CI/CD: Automation for Efficiency:**
   - ○ **Automated Testing:**
     - Implement automated tests to validate model performance.

- ○ **Automated Deployment:**
  - ■ Automate the deployment process.
- ○ **Infrastructure as Code:**
  - ■ Manage infrastructure using code.

Tools and Technologies: The Arsenal of Monitoring and Maintenance:

- **Cloud Monitoring Services:** AWS CloudWatch, Google Cloud Monitoring, Azure Monitor.
- **Logging Services:** ELK stack, Splunk, Datadog.
- **Monitoring Platforms:** Prometheus, Grafana, Datadog.
- **MLOps Platforms:** MLflow, Cubeflow, Seldon Core, SageMaker Pipelines, Vertex AI Pipelines, Azure Machine Learning Pipelines.

- **Data Drift Detection Tools:** Evidently AI, Arize AI, Fiddler AI.[17]

Best Practices: The Pillars of Success:

- **Define Clear KPIs:** Establish measurable KPIs.[18]
- **Automate Monitoring:** Reduce manual effort.
- **Establish a Baseline:** Detect deviations.[19]
- **Implement a Feedback Loop:** Collect user feedback.
- **Document Everything:** Maintain thorough documentation.
- **Regular Review and Update:** Adapt to changing conditions.

By embracing robust monitoring and maintenance practices, organizations can ensure that their deployed machine learning models deliver sustained value, adapt to evolving environments, and remain reliable assets.[20]

CHAPTER 14

Ethical Considerations in Machine Learning

Machine learning, while transformative, presents significant ethical challenges that demand careful consideration.[1] Building and deploying responsible AI systems requires a deep understanding of potential biases, privacy concerns, and the need for transparency.[2]

14.1 Bias and Fairness in Machine Learning Models

Bias in machine learning occurs when models systematically discriminate against certain groups or individuals based on sensitive attributes like race, gender, or religion.[3] Fairness aims to mitigate these biases and ensure equitable outcomes.[4]

Sources of Bias:

- **Data Bias:**
  - **Historical Bias:** Reflecting existing societal biases in the training data.[5]
  - **Sampling Bias:** Occurring when the training data is not representative of the population.[6]
  - **Measurement Bias:** Arising from inaccuracies or inconsistencies in data collection.[7]
- **Algorithmic Bias:**
  - **Bias in Model Selection:** Choosing models that inherently favor certain groups.
  - **Bias in Feature Engineering:** Creating features that encode discriminatory information.

- ○ **Bias in Optimization:** Optimizing for objectives that perpetuate existing inequalities.[8]

Fairness Metrics:

- **Statistical Parity:** Ensuring that different groups have equal probabilities of positive outcomes.[9]
- **Equal Opportunity:** Ensuring that different groups have equal probabilities of true positive outcomes.
- **Equalized Odds:** Ensuring that different groups have equal probabilities of both true positive and false positive outcomes.[10]
- **Predictive Parity:** Ensuring that the positive predictive values are equal across groups.

Mitigation Techniques:

- **Data Preprocessing:**
  - **Bias Detection:** Identifying and quantifying biases in the training data.[11]
  - **Data Augmentation:** Increasing the representation of underrepresented groups.[12]
  - **Reweighing:** Adjusting the weights of training samples to balance class distributions.
- **Algorithmic Modifications:**
  - **Adversarial Debiasing:** Training models to be invariant to sensitive attributes.
  - **Fairness Constraints:** Incorporating fairness metrics into the model's loss function.[13]
  - **Post-Processing:** Adjusting model outputs to achieve desired fairness properties.

14.2 Data Privacy and Security

Machine learning models often rely on vast amounts of personal data, raising significant privacy and security concerns.[14]

Privacy Risks:

- **Data Leakage:** Unauthorized access to or disclosure of sensitive data.
- **Re-identification:** Identifying individuals from anonymized datasets.
- **Inference Attacks:** Deducing sensitive information from model outputs.

Privacy-Preserving Techniques:

- **Differential Privacy:** Adding noise to data or model outputs to protect individual privacy.[15]

- **Federated Learning:** Training models on decentralized data sources without sharing raw data.[16]
- **Homomorphic Encryption:** Performing computations on encrypted data without decryption.[17]
- **Secure Multi-Party Computation (SMPC):** Enabling multiple parties to jointly compute a function without revealing their private inputs.[18]

Security Considerations:

- **Adversarial Attacks:** Manipulating input data to deceive machine learning models.[19]
- **Model Inversion Attacks:** Reconstructing training data from model parameters.[20]
- **Supply Chain Security:** Ensuring the integrity and security of machine learning components.

14.3 Interpretability and Explainability of Machine Learning Models

Interpretability and explainability are crucial for building trust in machine learning models and ensuring their responsible use.

Interpretability:

- The degree to which a human can understand the cause of a decision.
- Relevant when the model itself is simple, like a linear model.

Explainability:

- The degree to which a human can understand the cause of a decision, even when the model is complex.
- Crucial for complex models like deep neural networks.

Techniques for Interpretability and Explainability:

- **Feature Importance:** Identifying the most influential features in a model's predictions.
- **SHAP (SHapley Additive exPlanations):** Assigning importance values to features based on game theory.
- **LIME (Local Interpretable Model-agnostic Explanations):** Approximating complex models with simpler, interpretable models locally.
- **Attention Mechanisms:** Visualizing the parts of the input that the model focuses on.
- **Rule Extraction:** Extracting human-readable rules from machine learning models.

Benefits of Interpretability and Explainability:

- **Building Trust:** Increasing confidence in model predictions.
- **Debugging Models:** Identifying and correcting errors in model behavior.[21]
- **Improving Models:** Gaining insights into model weaknesses and areas for improvement.
- **Ensuring Fairness:** Detecting and mitigating biases in model predictions.
- **Meeting Regulatory Requirements:** Complying with regulations that require explainable AI.

14.4 Responsible AI Development and Deployment

Responsible AI development and deployment involves adopting ethical principles and practices throughout the machine learning lifecycle.[22]

Key Principles:

- **Fairness:** Ensuring equitable outcomes for all groups.[23]
- **Accountability:** Establishing clear lines of responsibility for model decisions.
- **Transparency:** Providing clear and understandable explanations of model behavior.
- **Privacy:** Protecting sensitive data and respecting user privacy.[24]
- **Safety:** Preventing unintended consequences and ensuring model robustness.
- **Human Control:** Maintaining human oversight and control over AI systems.

Best Practices:

- **Ethical Guidelines:** Establishing ethical guidelines for AI development and deployment.

- **Impact Assessments:** Conducting impact assessments to identify potential risks and benefits.
- **Stakeholder Engagement:** Engaging with stakeholders to understand their concerns and perspectives.
- **Continuous Monitoring:** Monitoring model performance and identifying potential biases.[25]
- **Auditing and Certification:** Conducting independent audits and certifications to ensure compliance with ethical standards.

14.5 Case Studies of Ethical Challenges in Machine Learning

Real-world case studies highlight the ethical challenges and potential consequences of biased or irresponsible AI.

Examples:

- **COMPAS (Correctional Offender Management Profiling for Alternative Sanctions):** A risk assessment tool used in the US criminal justice system that was found to be biased against African Americans.[26]
- **Amazon's AI Recruiting Tool:** A recruiting tool that was found to be biased against women.[27]
- **Facial Recognition Technology:** Facial recognition systems that have been shown to be less accurate for people of color.[28]
- **Social Media Algorithms:** Algorithms that amplify misinformation and hate speech.[29]
- **Autonomous Vehicles:** Ethical dilemmas related to accident scenarios and decision-making.[30]

Lessons Learned:

- Bias is pervasive and can have significant consequences.[31]
- Data privacy and security are paramount.
- Interpretability and explainability are essential for building trust.
- Responsible AI development requires a multidisciplinary approach.
- Continuous monitoring and evaluation are crucial.

By addressing these ethical considerations, we can harness the power of machine learning to create a more equitable, just, and responsible future.

CHAPTER 15

Advanced Topics and Future Trends in Machine Learning

Machine learning is a rapidly evolving field, with continuous advancements pushing the boundaries of what's possible.[1] This chapter explores some of the most exciting and impactful areas of research and development.

15.1 Reinforcement Learning: Concepts and Applications

Reinforcement learning is a paradigm where an agent learns to make decisions by interacting with an environment.[2] The agent receives rewards or penalties based on its actions,[4] and its goal is to maximize the cumulative reward.[5]

Key Concepts:

- **Agent:** The decision-making entity that interacts with the environment.[6]
- **Environment:** The external world with which the agent interacts.
- **State:** The current situation or context of the agent.
- **Action:** A decision made by the agent.[7]
- **Reward:** A signal indicating the desirability of an action.[8]
- **Policy:** A strategy that maps states to actions.[9]
- **Value Function:** A function that estimates the expected cumulative reward from a state.[10]

RL Algorithms:

- **Q-Learning:** A value-based algorithm that learns an optimal policy by estimating the Q-values (action-value function).[11]

- **Deep Q-Networks (DQNs):** Using deep neural networks to approximate Q-values.[12]
- **Policy Gradient Methods:** Directly optimizing the policy using gradient descent.[13]
- **Actor-Critic Methods:** Combining value-based and policy-based approaches.[14]
- **Proximal Policy Optimization (PPO):** A state-of-the-art policy gradient algorithm.

Applications:

- **Game Playing:** Mastering complex games like Go and Atari.[15]
- **Robotics:** Controlling robots to perform tasks in dynamic environments.[16]
- **Autonomous Driving:** Developing self-driving cars that can navigate complex traffic scenarios.[17]

- **Resource Management:** Optimizing resource allocation in data centers or power grids.[18]
- **Recommendation Systems:** Personalizing recommendations based on user interactions.[19]
- **Healthcare:** Developing personalized treatment plans or drug discovery.[20]

15.2 Generative Adversarial Networks (GANs): Generating Realistic Data

Generative Adversarial Networks (GANs) are a class of generative models that learn to generate realistic data by pitting two neural networks against each other: a generator and a discriminator.[21]

Key Concepts:

- **Generator:** A neural network that generates synthetic data samples.[22]
- **Discriminator:** A neural network that distinguishes between real and generated data samples.[23]
- **Adversarial Training:** The generator and discriminator are trained simultaneously in a competitive manner.[24]
- **Loss Function:** The generator aims to minimize the discriminator's ability to distinguish between real and generated data, while the discriminator aims to maximize its ability to distinguish.

GAN Architectures:

- **Deep Convolutional GANs (DCGANs):** Using convolutional neural networks for image generation.
- **Conditional GANs (CGANs):** Generating data samples conditioned on specific inputs.

- **StyleGANs:** Generating highly realistic and controllable images.
- **CycleGANs:** Performing image-to-image translation without paired training data.[25]

Applications:

- **Image Generation:** Creating realistic images, videos, and 3D models.
- **Image Editing:** Modifying images in a realistic way.[26]
- **Text-to-Image Synthesis:** Generating images from textual descriptions.[27]
- **Data Augmentation:** Generating synthetic data to improve model training.[28]
- **Anomaly Detection:** Identifying unusual data samples.[29]
- **Drug Discovery:** Generating novel drug candidates.[30]

15.3 AutoML: Automating Machine Learning Workflows

AutoML aims to automate the end-to-end machine learning process, from data preprocessing to model deployment.[31]

Key Components:

- **Data Preprocessing:** Automating data cleaning, feature engineering, and feature selection.[32]
- **Model Selection:** Automatically selecting the best model from a set of candidate models.[33]
- **Hyperparameter Tuning:** Automatically optimizing model hyperparameters.
- **Model Evaluation:** Automatically evaluating model performance.[34]
- **Model Deployment:** Automating the deployment of trained models.

Benefits:

- **Increased Productivity:** Reducing the time and effort required to build and deploy machine learning models.
- **Democratization of AI:** Making machine learning accessible to non-experts.[35]
- **Improved Model Performance:** Finding optimal model configurations automatically.

Tools and Platforms:

- **Auto-sklearn:** An AutoML toolkit for scikit-learn models.[36]
- **TPOT (Tree-based Pipeline Optimization Tool):** An AutoML tool that uses genetic programming to optimize machine learning pipelines.[37]
- **Google Cloud AutoML:** A suite of AutoML services for various tasks.

- **Microsoft Azure AutoML:** An AutoML service for building and deploying machine learning models.

15.4 Quantum Machine Learning: Exploring the Future of Computation

Quantum machine learning combines quantum computing and machine learning to develop algorithms that can leverage the power of quantum computers.[38]

Key Concepts:

- **Quantum Computing:** Using quantum phenomena like superposition and entanglement to perform computations.[39]
- **Quantum Algorithms:** Algorithms designed to run on quantum computers.[40]

- **Quantum Neural Networks:** Neural networks that operate on quantum data.[41]
- **Variational Quantum Eigensolver (VQE):** An algorithm for finding the ground state of a quantum system.
- **Quantum Support Vector Machines (QSVMs):** Quantum algorithms for classification tasks.[42]

Potential Benefits:

- **Speedup:** Solving certain machine learning problems exponentially faster than classical computers.
- **Increased Capacity:** Handling larger and more complex datasets.
- **Improved Accuracy:** Achieving higher accuracy in certain tasks.

Challenges:

- **Hardware Limitations:** Quantum computers are still in their early stages of development.[43]
- **Algorithm Development:** Developing efficient quantum machine learning algorithms is challenging.
- **Data Encoding:** Encoding classical data into quantum states can be complex.

15.5 Emerging Trends and Research Directions in Machine Learning

Machine learning research is constantly evolving, with new trends and directions emerging.

Key Trends:

- **Explainable AI (XAI):** Developing techniques to make machine learning models more transparent and interpretable.

- **Federated Learning:** Training models on decentralized data sources without sharing raw data.[44]
- **Self-Supervised Learning:** Learning from unlabeled data by creating pretext tasks.
- **Graph Neural Networks (GNNs):** Processing and analyzing graph-structured data.[45]
- **Transformers:** Revolutionizing natural language processing and computer vision.[46]
- **Meta-Learning:** Learning to learn, enabling models to adapt to new tasks quickly.
- **Reinforcement Learning from Human Feedback (RLHF):** Improving model alignment with human preferences.[47]
- **Foundation Models:** Large-scale models that can be adapted to a wide range of tasks.[48]

- **AI Ethics and Safety:** Addressing the ethical and societal implications of AI.
- **AI for Science:** Applying AI to accelerate scientific discovery.

Research Directions:

- **Developing more robust and efficient algorithms.**
- **Improving model generalization and robustness to adversarial attacks.**
- **Developing AI systems that can reason and understand causality.**
- **Creating AI systems that can learn and adapt in real-time.**
- **Developing AI systems that can interact with humans in a natural and intuitive way.**
- **Exploring the intersection of AI and other fields, such as biology, physics, and medicine.**

By staying abreast of these advanced topics and emerging trends, you can gain a deeper understanding of the future of machine learning and contribute to its continued advancement.

Conclusion: Navigating the Machine Learning Landscape

As we conclude our exploration of machine learning, it's essential to reflect on the journey, synthesize the core concepts, and envision the future trajectory of this transformative field.

Summarizing Key Learnings and Insights:

Our journey through machine learning has equipped us with a robust understanding of its foundational principles and practical applications. We've traversed a landscape spanning from the basics of data preprocessing to the complexities of deep learning and advanced topics.

1. Foundational Principles:

- **Data-Driven Approach:** Machine learning thrives on data, emphasizing the importance of data collection, preprocessing, and feature engineering.
- **Algorithm Diversity:** We've explored a wide array of algorithms, from linear regression and decision trees to neural networks and reinforcement learning, each suited to different problem domains.
- **Model Evaluation:** Rigorous evaluation techniques, including cross-validation and various performance metrics, are crucial for ensuring model reliability and generalization.
- **Hyperparameter Tuning:** Optimizing model performance through hyperparameter tuning is a vital aspect of practical machine learning.

- **Ethical Considerations:** The ethical implications of machine learning, including bias, fairness, privacy, and interpretability, demand careful consideration.

2. Practical Applications:

- **Supervised Learning:** We've applied supervised learning to classification and regression tasks, building models that predict outcomes based on labeled data.
- **Unsupervised Learning:** We've explored unsupervised learning techniques like clustering and dimensionality reduction to uncover hidden patterns and structures in unlabeled data.
- **Natural Language Processing (NLP):** We've delved into NLP techniques for text preprocessing, representation, sentiment analysis, and topic modeling.

- **Computer Vision:** We've explored computer vision techniques for image processing, feature extraction, object detection, and image classification.
- **Time Series Analysis:** We've applied time series analysis and forecasting methods to predict future values based on historical data.
- **Recommender Systems:** We've built recommender systems using collaborative and content-based filtering to personalize user experiences.
- **Model Deployment:** We've learned to package, deploy, monitor, and maintain machine learning models in production environments.

3. Advanced Topics and Future Trends:

- **Reinforcement Learning:** We've explored the potential of reinforcement learning for developing intelligent agents that can learn through interaction with environments.

- **Generative Adversarial Networks (GANs):** We've witnessed the power of GANs in generating realistic data and performing creative tasks.
- **AutoML:** We've seen how AutoML is automating machine learning workflows, making AI more accessible.
- **Quantum Machine Learning:** We've glimpsed the potential of quantum computing to revolutionize machine learning.
- **Emerging Trends:** We've discussed the latest research directions, including explainable AI, federated learning, and AI ethics.

The Future of Machine Learning and Its Impact

Machine learning is poised to reshape industries and societies in profound ways. Its impact will be felt across various domains:

- **Healthcare:** Personalized medicine, drug discovery, and medical imaging.
- **Transportation:** Autonomous vehicles, traffic management, and logistics optimization.
- **Finance:** Fraud detection, risk assessment, and algorithmic trading.
- **Manufacturing:** Predictive maintenance, quality control, and robotic automation.
- **Education:** Personalized learning, adaptive tutoring, and educational analytics.

- **Environment:** Climate modeling, resource management, and conservation efforts.
- **Scientific Discovery:** Accelerated research in fields like physics, biology, and materials science.

Key Trends Shaping the Future:

- **AI Democratization:** Making AI tools and techniques more accessible to a wider audience.
- **AI Ethics and Governance:** Establishing ethical guidelines and regulations for AI development and deployment.
- **AI Explainability and Transparency:** Building AI systems that are more interpretable and understandable.
- **AI Collaboration:** Fostering collaboration between humans and AI systems.

- **AI for Social Good:** Applying AI to address pressing social and environmental challenges.

Continuing Your Machine Learning Journey

Machine learning is a lifelong learning endeavor. To continue your journey, consider the following:

- **Deepen Your Knowledge:** Explore advanced topics and specialized domains within machine learning.
- **Practice Consistently:** Build projects, participate in competitions, and contribute to open-source initiatives.
- **Stay Updated:** Follow research publications, attend conferences, and engage with the machine learning community.

- **Embrace Lifelong Learning:** Machine learning is a rapidly evolving field, so continuous learning is essential.
- **Focus on Ethical AI:** Prioritize ethical considerations in your machine learning work.
- **Specialize:** Focus on a specific area of machine learning that interests you, such as computer vision, NLP, or reinforcement learning.
- **Contribute:** Share your knowledge and expertise by writing blog posts, creating tutorials, or giving presentations.
- **Network:** Connect with other machine learning practitioners and researchers.

Final Thoughts:

Machine learning is a powerful tool with the potential to create a better future. By embracing ethical principles, fostering collaboration, and committing to continuous learning, we can harness the transformative power of AI for the benefit of all. The journey of machine learning is one of constant discovery and innovation. Embrace the challenges, celebrate the successes, and contribute to the ongoing evolution of this remarkable field.

Appendix

This appendix serves as a valuable resource for reinforcing your understanding and facilitating your continued growth in machine learning.

A.1 Python Libraries Quick Reference

Python's ecosystem provides a rich set of libraries that are essential for machine learning practitioners.

- **NumPy:**
  - ○ Fundamental package for numerical computing.
  - ○ Provides efficient array operations, linear algebra, and random number generation.
  - ○ Key functions: numpy.array(), numpy.dot(), numpy.mean(), numpy.random.
- **Pandas:**
  - ○ Library for data manipulation and analysis.
  - ○ Provides data structures like DataFrames and Series.
  - ○ Key functions: pandas.read_csv(), pandas.DataFrame(), pandas.groupby(), pandas.merge().
- **Scikit-learn (sklearn):**
  - ○ Comprehensive library for machine learning algorithms.
  - ○ Provides tools for classification, regression, clustering,

dimensionality reduction, and model evaluation.

- ○ Key modules: sklearn.linear_model, sklearn.tree, sklearn.cluster, sklearn.metrics.

- **Matplotlib:**
  - ○ Library for creating static, interactive, and animated visualizations.
  - ○ Key functions: matplotlib.pyplot.plot(), matplotlib.pyplot.scatter(), matplotlib.pyplot.imshow().

- **Seaborn:**
  - ○ Library for statistical data visualization, built on top of Matplotlib.
  - ○ Provides high-level interfaces for creating informative and attractive plots.
  - ○ Key functions: seaborn.histplot(),

seaborn.boxplot(),
seaborn.heatmap().

- **TensorFlow:**
  - Open-source machine learning framework for building and training deep learning models.
  - Provides tools for defining and optimizing neural networks.
- **Keras:**
  - High-level neural networks API that runs on top of TensorFlow.
  - Simplifies the process of building and training deep learning models.
- **PyTorch:**
  - Another popular deep learning framework that allows for dynamic computation graphs.
  - Popular in research.
- **NLTK (Natural Language Toolkit):**
  - Library for natural language processing tasks.

- Provides tools for tokenization, stemming, lemmatization, and text classification.
- **spaCy:**
  - Advanced library for natural language processing, that is very fast.
- **OpenCV (cv2):**
  - Library for computer vision and image processing.
  - Provides tools for image manipulation, feature extraction, and object detection.
- **Joblib:**
  - Library for efficient serialization of python objects, especially large numpy arrays.
- **Pickle:**
  - Standard python library for object serialization.

A.2 Mathematical Foundations for Machine Learning

A solid understanding of mathematics is essential for comprehending and applying machine learning algorithms.

- **Linear Algebra:**
    - Vectors and matrices: Representing data and transformations.
    - Matrix operations: Addition, multiplication, transposition, inversion.
    - Eigenvalues and eigenvectors: Understanding data transformations and dimensionality reduction.
    - Singular Value Decomposition (SVD): Matrix factorization.
- **Calculus:**

- Derivatives: Optimizing model parameters using gradient descent.
- Partial derivatives: Optimizing functions with multiple variables.
- Gradient descent: Iterative optimization algorithm.
- Chain rule: Calculating derivatives of composite functions.

- **Probability and Statistics:**
  - Probability distributions: Modeling data and uncertainty.
  - Statistical inference: Drawing conclusions from data.
  - Hypothesis testing: Evaluating the significance of results.
  - Bayesian statistics: Updating beliefs based on evidence.

- **Optimization:**
  - Convex optimization: Finding global minima of convex functions.

- Gradient-based optimization: Using gradients to minimize loss functions.
- Loss functions: Measuring the error between predicted and actual values.

A.3 Datasets and Resources for Practice

Practice is crucial for mastering machine learning.

- **Datasets:**
  - UCI Machine Learning Repository: A collection of diverse datasets.
  - Kaggle Datasets: A platform for sharing and exploring datasets.
  - Scikit-learn Datasets: Built-in datasets for practice.

- Tensorflow Datasets: Large collection of datasets.
- Huggingface Datasets: Large collection of datasets, especially for NLP.
- **Platforms:**
  - Kaggle: A platform for machine learning competitions and datasets.
  - Coursera: Offers online courses and specializations in machine learning.
  - edX: Provides online courses and programs from top universities.
  - Fast.ai: Offers practical deep learning courses.
  - Deeplearning.ai: Offers deep learning specialization courses.
- **Books:**
  - "Hands-On Machine Learning with Scikit-Learn, Keras & TensorFlow" by Aurélien Géron.

- "Deep Learning" by Ian Goodfellow, Yoshua Bengio, and Aaron Courville.
- "Pattern Recognition and Machine Learning" by Christopher M. Bishop.[1]

- **Blogs and Websites:**
  - Towards Data Science: A Medium publication with articles on data science and machine learning.
  - Machine Learning Mastery: A blog with practical tutorials and guides.
  - Papers With Code: A website that tracks machine learning research papers.

A.4 Troubleshooting Common Machine Learning Errors

Encountering errors is a natural part of the machine learning process.

- **Data Preprocessing Errors:**
  - Missing values: Impute or remove missing values.
  - Outliers: Identify and handle outliers.
  - Data scaling: Scale or normalize data.
- **Model Training Errors:**
  - Overfitting: Use regularization, dropout, or early stopping.
  - Underfitting: Increase model complexity or feature engineering.
  - Convergence issues: Adjust learning rate or optimization algorithm.
- **Evaluation Errors:**

- Imbalanced datasets: Use appropriate evaluation metrics or resampling techniques.
- Incorrect cross-validation: Use stratified or time series cross-validation.
- Data leakage: Ensure that training and testing data are properly separated.
- **Deployment Errors:**
  - Model serialization issues: Use correct serialization/deserialization methods.
  - API errors: Check API endpoints and data formats.
  - Containerization issues: Verify Dockerfile and container configuration.
- **General recommendations:**
  - Read error messages carefully.
  - Use debugging tools.
  - Search for solutions online.
  - Consult documentation.

A.5 Glossary of Terms

- **Algorithm:** A set of rules or instructions for solving a problem.
- **Artificial Intelligence (AI):** The simulation of human intelligence processes by machines.
- **Backpropagation:** An algorithm for training neural networks by propagating error gradients.
- **Bias:** A systematic error that favors certain outcomes.
- **Classification:** A supervised learning task that predicts categorical labels.
- **Clustering:** An unsupervised learning task that groups similar data points.
- **Convolutional Neural Network (CNN):** A neural network architecture for image processing.
- **Data Drift:** A change in the statistical properties of the input data.

- **Deep Learning:** A subfield of machine learning that uses deep neural networks.
- **Feature Engineering:** The process of creating and selecting relevant features.
- **Gradient Descent:** An optimization algorithm for minimizing loss functions.
- **Hyperparameter:** A parameter that is set before training a model.
- **Loss Function:** A function that measures the error between predicted and actual values.
- **Machine Learning (ML):** A field of study that enables computers to learn from data.
- **Neural Network:** A computational model inspired by the structure of the human brain.
- **Overfitting:** A model that performs well on training data but poorly on unseen data.

- **Regression:** A supervised learning task that predicts continuous values.
- **Reinforcement Learning (RL):** A learning paradigm where an agent learns through interaction with an environment.
- **Supervised Learning:** A learning paradigm where models learn from labeled data.
- **Unsupervised Learning:** A learning paradigm where models learn from unlabeled data.
- **Validation Set:** A subset of data used to tune hyperparameters and monitor model performance.
- **Variance:** The variability of a model's predictions for different training datasets.

www.ingramcontent.com/pod-product-compliance
Lightning Source LLC
LaVergne TN
LVHW051427050326
832903LV00030BD/2952